THE MASSACHUSETTS CHRONICLES

THE HISTORY OF MASSACHUSETTS FROM EARLIEST TIMES TO THE PRESENT DAY

"As we celebrate Massachusetts' storied past, we are grateful that the legacy program of Plymouth 400 has produced these Chronicles that chart the Commonwealth's remarkable history. These stories, written from all perspectives, are designed to educate our students and strengthen our sense of community as we look ahead to the future."

Charles D. Baker
Governor of Massachusetts

"The freedom that protects all our other freedoms is free speech, which is part of the First Amendment."

January 14, 2020

"As we commemorate 400 years of history, nothing is more important than rediscovering the rich diversity and the highs and lows of our collective past. These wonderful chronicles of the Massachusetts story do just that. They make the past accessible to everyone."

Michele Pecoraro
*Executive Director,
Plymouth 400*

Frederick W. Clark Jr.
*President, Bridgewater
State University*

Dr. Gary Maestas
*Superintendent,
Plymouth Public Schools*

PLYMOUTH 400™
1620-2020

BRIDGEWATER
STATE UNIVERSITY

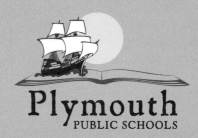

Plymouth
PUBLIC SCHOOLS

THE MASSACHUSETTS CHRONICLES

NEW YEAR PREPARATIONS UNDERWAY

**By our Wampanoag eye in the sky,
Flying Eagle** Planting Moon Time, 1613

RUNNERS HAVE been traveling throughout Wampanoag Territory, visiting all villages to check on preparations for new year ceremonies. Families from each of the 69 villages have completed the move from winter homes to their summer planting fields. Runners report certain Manomet families consulted with their sachem, or leader, regarding the planting fields he had designated, concerned they had not lain fallow long enough to ensure good soil for corn. After some discussion, the sachem agreed to assign them different fields.

Many men will be busy in the cedar swamps, collecting saplings for new house frames. The past winter gave just enough snow and rain, and the swamps are not too deep with water and spring melt. As the men make holes in which to set the frame poles, children watch their grandparents peel bark from the cut trees and separate the inner and outer layers. Little hands may try this

work, learning as they watch their elders that not even the smallest twig will be wasted. No one forgets that the trees have given their lives so we may have shelter, materials for our baskets and mats, and the green fronds for offerings in prayer. Their sacrifice is honored with thanksgiving and ceremony.

Every spring, in accordance with ancient tradition, people give thanks for the new life that comes forth: for the flowers that bloom even before the snow leaves the ground; for the tiny leaves of the oak that tell us there will be no more frost, and it is time to plant; for all the new fawns, baby rabbits, squirrels, and turkeys; for the herring and salmon that swim

THE WAMPANOAG people have lived in what is now southeastern Massachusetts for more than 12,000 years. By the 1600s there were as many as 100,000 people living in 69 villages, which comprised the Wampanoag Nation. When the *Mayflower* Pilgrims landed in what is now Provincetown in 1620, they were in the territory of Meeshawm of the Wampanoag Nation.

upriver to bear their young; and for our plant relatives that give us food and medicine. We especially remember the white pine, who the ancestor Creator made us from.

Ceremonies begin at first light on the day of the new moon, and the thanksgiving to all life will commence. Runners have reported to the sachem's councils that all preparations are well underway. The planting fields have been burned over and the earth of old corn mounds turned to bury the ashes. Each village is joyous with feast preparations (not to mention the warmer weather!), as the women reach into the remaining stores of corn and beans. Some folks may even have some dried squash or pumpkin left to share. Spring brings plenty of fresh herring (often used to fertilize our land), flounder, clams, quahogs, and other food from the sea. Fresh greens sprout in abundance. And every hearth will certainly have a turkey roasting, or a large cod or bluefish.

As new year observances conclude, the women will begin preparations for this year's planting ceremonies. This article is offered in thanksgiving to all my relations.

SACHEMS MEET AFTER DISAPPEARANCES

By our investigative reporter, Running Fox
Time of Green Corn, 1614

EARLIER IN THE summer, runners reported that after another ship came to trade, 20 men from communities on the narrow land simply disappeared. Families are frantic over the loss of their loved ones. Now Tisquantum and six others have gone missing from Patuxet.

It is unimaginable that sailors would so brazenly take even more people. Ships have been coming to our country for 100 years. What manner of people steal others from their homes?

Parents are left without sons, wives without husbands, children without fathers, and siblings without brothers that only a day ago were here. All communities are in shock.

Massipee will host the sachems of all coastal villages to examine these horrific incidents. Before this conference, they will consult their elders' and warriors' councils, and also nations up the coast with experience of ships coming into their territory. Sachems will establish new protocols for exchange with these strangers from afar to secure our people's safety in the homeland.

TISQUANTUM (also known as Squanto) spoke English because he and 26 others had been kidnapped in 1614, taken to England, and sold into slavery. After five years, he made it back home, only to find his village of Patuxet wiped out by plague. Consider his state of mind: suffering the trauma of kidnap and slavery, finally getting home only to find his entire village wiped out by disease. The Pilgrims viewed him as their aide and translator, while some of his own saw him as a traitor. Squanto died of a fever in 1622.

LAND OF OPPORTUNITY

By our pamphleteer, London, England
December 31, 1616

NEW ENGLAND is the perfect place to make a new and prosperous life in North America, according to Captain John Smith. You may have heard of Smith, as he is known to be an early leader of the first lasting English colony in North America at Jamestown, Virginia.

After recent voyages to explore its magnificent coast, Captain Smith is promoting the region as the ideal location for settlement. He has named it "New England" and published a map of the coastal area containing English place-names, some of which were provided by Prince Charles, son of King James I of England.

For years, European seafarers have been fishing the waters off Cape Cod and the rest of New England, the homeland of Native Americans, but no one from Europe has so far established a colony there. Smith believes there are huge opportunities for agriculture, industry, and commerce such as fishing, farming, and fur-trading.

While the Captain failed to find gold on his earlier expeditions, any Englishman who settles there will become master and owner of his own labor and land. With hard work, colonists will quickly grow rich. But reaping the rewards will mean risking their lives to survive wild animals and harsh winters.

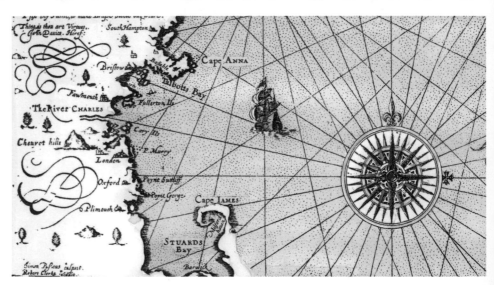

Native people are numerous in New England. According to reports, they live together in villages, cultivating corn and other crops. Chiefs, known as sachems, are responsible for

LONG BEFORE the explorer Christopher Columbus, Norseman Leif Erikson visited North America's northeastern coast, as one of the first Europeans to set foot on the continent. Did he ever reach Cape Cod? In 1497, John Cabot claimed North America's Atlantic lands for England's Henry VII. Virginia, named for the "Virgin Queen" Elizabeth I, was the first of what would become Britain's 13 colonies in North America.

assigning planting areas to the families. They inhabit two homes—one near the coast in summer, the other sheltered inland in winter—but there are no fences to close off lands and make them private property. Their land is owned by the community. Unlike Europeans, they consider the land to be everyone's and not as property to be divided up and privately owned.

This land is said to be rich with raw materials, ideal for settlement. These include giant trees, perfect for making houses and ships. The Native people's lack of interest in land ownership, and the absence of any kind of legal system, make this place a perfect prospect for establishing property rights and growing rich.

Deadly disease from ships kills entire villages

By our freelance reporter, Voice of the Wind
End of Winter Moon, 1619

THE GREAT sickness sweeping across our land these last two years is finally relenting! The oldest among us do not remember such death and fear! Disease rampaged mercilessly from the north, and everyone in 40 of our villages is gone.

Elders and the weak were taken, with people of all ages, even children and infants, becoming sick and dying within three days. Those who survived fled to relatives in living villages, praying the sickness did not follow. No one was left to bury the dead, and their bones lay strewn across the land.

Runners from the northern nations inform us that this disease came with ships from across the water. They too have lost thousands to this horrid death. Entire communities are gone, and with them generations of knowledge and wisdom.

The prayers and ceremonies of the Medicine people had no effect. This has terrified communities, as nothing like this has ever been known to happen.

Sachems, councils, and clan mothers still among us are coming together to formulate the rebuilding of our nation. We must carry on our responsibilities as the people of this land.

AMONG THE Indigenous nations of what is now New England, one method of delivering important news and information was by using young men as runners to carry messages. They were often able to run 90 to 100 miles per day — that's the equivalent of going from Hyannis to Boston!

MYSTERY SHIP ARRIVES
THIS TIME IT LOOKS LIKE THEY MEAN TO STAY

By our freelance reporter, Voice of the Wind
Winter Moon, 1620

ONE MORE SHIP has come to our shores, but it is very different this time. Women and children are among the group, and the men have begun to build on the grounds of Patuxet. Runners are reporting their movements to the sachems, who express their concern at this recent occurrence.

Our nations on the coast, as well as those along the river ways, have seen many, many ships come and go over the last 100 years. They have fished in our waters, sought out those who would trade furs and goods with them, and they have wandered about our lands, noting the different kinds of animals, plants, and locations of springs, ponds, and rivers. While we watched and remained aware of the places they traveled, we also realized that they would be returning to their own countries.

Then the day came that their visits were not so seemingly benign, but took a darker turn. This was with the kidnappings of so many of our young men from coastal villages. With the exceptions of Tisquantum and Epenow from Aquinnah, there was never even one report of any who returned home. They were gone forever, leaving their families coldly without their loved ones.

In the past, the ships always left at the end of summer. These people are clearly intent on staying. What changes will be coming now that we must contend with? Our people are still exhausted and fearful as a result of the great sickness. Many have feelings of foreboding about this arrival, and rightly so for a number of reasons.

While ceremonies for the dead have been performed, we of the living do not go back to the places where so many died, but leave it to Earth and time to effect healing. We have placed many new memory holes to aid us in remembering those of Patuxet and the other villages where everyone was lost in the great dying.

This new group has also not approached nor paid respect to any of our present leaders. They have come into our territory and started building their homes with not the slightest regard for the protocols of entry into our nation. They have not gained permission to come here and live in our land, and yet behave as if their actions should be acceptable to people.

What causes these people to behave in such a manner? Many villages that are left from the great sickness have joined with Massasoit of Pokanoket, and the councils have begun discussions. While still grappling with rebuilding our nation after the great dying, decisions must also be made as to how we treat these intruders into our country.

A RELIGIOUS group with roots in Nottinghamshire and Yorkshire in England believed it necessary to separate from the Church of England. Persecuted in England, these Separatists moved to Holland, where they lived for more than a decade—at first in Amsterdam and then in Leiden. They moved to North America in 1620 to start anew, supported, so they believed, by the will of God.

EPIC JOURNEY TO A NEW LIFE

AFTER making landfall last month, our small group of pilgrims has survived our first encounter with Native people. We give thanks to God for our deliverance!

Our sailing ship *Mayflower* has safely brought us to New England, our new homeland, where we will be free to practice our religion as we please, and make a new life so that we can prosper.

Sick and weary after weeks at sea, we came to anchor in a good harbor and pleasant bay more than three weeks ago.

The women came ashore to do the laundry as they had great need for washing. The men unloaded and repaired our shallop—a longboat that can be rowed or fitted with a mast and sails.

By our *Mayflower* writer on Cape Cod
December 9, 1620

Led by Myles Standish, our military adviser, 16 armed men—myself included—later went ashore to explore the bay side of Cape Cod, and had our first glimpse of Native people who ran off as we approached.

It is not surprising they have decided to keep their distance. Not so long ago some were kidnapped by English seafarers, and sold into slavery.

But our group is not like those who have gone before: we have brought women and children, and it is clear we mean to stay—by establishing a permanent settlement for our people.

Many who accompanied us on the voyage are not Separatists like us. Some were unhappy that without a royal charter or patent, there could be no official authority governing our colony.

We put their minds at rest by drawing up a "Mayflower Compact" while still aboard the ship. A group of men signed the document which creates a representative government, binding us together for the common good.

As yet, we have failed to find a possible settlement site, although we have discovered harvested fields. Beneath heaps of sand, we found baskets of corn which we decided to take for ourselves.

Amid freezing cold winter temperatures, we are desperate to

survive, but God will judge us for this theft. If we can track the people who buried the corn, we must surely compensate them for their loss.

Setting out in the shallop, we discovered a place like a grave. We dug it up and later covered it back over. We also came upon domed houses that Native people had clearly left in a hurry. They contained clay pots and wooden bowls, and we decided to take some of the best things.

On our last exploration, we were confronted by at least 30 Native men. Their cries terrified us as well as their arrows which came thick and fast around us. We responded with gunshots, and the warriors withdrew.

Now it is time to move on and find a better home.

**By our senior chronicler
in Plymouth Colony**
March 19, 1621

ENGLISH PLANT COLONY, CLEARLY MEAN TO STAY...

THANKS TO GOD'S mercy, our colony has survived the last winter in the fellowship of the Gospel, free to worship as we wish. Since arriving off Cape Cod from England, death has been everywhere, claiming the lives of about half the 102 souls who completed the voyage on our sailing ship, *Mayflower*. The wife of William Bradford, one of our leaders, was among them. Mercifully, others—including some women and most children—have been left untouched by illness.

We have chosen to make Plymouth our new coastal home. Exhausted and desperate, we found it impossible to continue our search for a better place to settle. Although the harbor is shallow, there is plentiful clean spring water.

It was not our plan to make for Cape Cod Bay, where Plymouth is located, as it was north of our intended destination.

Plymouth is named on a map, recently published by Captain John Smith, who explored the New England coast. It is coincidence that it is also the name of the English port from where we set sail for North America. Our new home is on the site of the former Wampanoag village of Patuxet. The Native people of Patuxet and other nearby villages were wiped out by an epidemic known as "the great dying."

We have erected wooden dwellings for shelter against the winter. For now, we are farming in common, but we know we will receive land eventually.

We have use of the land but do not fully own it. Our colony is co-owned by merchants in London, and we must wait seven years and pay off our debts before we can be sole owners and expand to settle other places.

Each of us has brought enough supplies to survive for a year, including clothing, tools,

household implements, and food. The men have muskets and swords.

We are concerned about threats from Native people, and have built a fort on a hill for our guns. With commanding views across the plain and the bay, it provides some basic protection.

Despite our fears, we are not without Native allies. A few days ago, a Native man called Samoset marched into the settlement and bade us welcome in English!

FOUNDED IN 1947 by Boston financier and archeologist Henry Hornblower II, Plimoth Plantation is a "living history" museum. The Wampanoag Homesite focuses on the ancient traditions and cultural survival of the region's Native people. In the 17th-century English Village, role-players represent the lives of actual residents of early Plymouth by speaking, acting, and dressing in the style of the 1620s. Museum exhibits also include *Mayflower*, a full-scale reproduction of the ship that brought the Pilgrims in 1620, and the Plimoth Grist Mill, a working, water-powered mill.

MASSASOIT MAKES HISTORIC ALLIANCE

MASSASOIT, also called Ousamequin, a leader of the Native Wampanoag people, yesterday completed a historic agreement with the English settlers of Plymouth Colony, *writes our senior chronicler, March 23, 1621*.

The Wampanoags, whose name means "People of the First Light," have made an alliance of mutual support with the small community of English Separatist settlers.

They have Tisquantum and Samoset to thank, acting as envoys for Massasoit, who

lives in a village called Pokanoket. Samoset, an Abenaki man, learned some English from visiting fishermen; Tisquantum or "Squanto," a Patuxet man, is fluent in English.

At a ceremony, the Plymouth Governor John Carver kissed the hand of Massasoit, who returned the honor.

Massasoit weighed the possibility of whether to ally with the Narragansett or the English. He has now made a calculated decision to side with the English. The

Wampanoag people inhabit the coastal areas where the settlers have chosen to make their colony. But they have been weakened by disease, struggling to defend themselves against the powerful Narragansett people, who have been largely unscathed by the epidemic of the great dying.

The settlers also see opportunity. They believe the agreement with the Wampanoag people provides the best chance of ensuring the colony's future prosperity.

COLONY SAYS THANKS FOR HEALTHY HARVEST

SETTLERS PRAISE THE LORD AFTER EPIC STRUGGLE

By our diarist in Plymouth
October 3, 1621

WE DREAMED about this moment. As we carefully gathered in our harvest, the Governor of our community declared that we rejoice and celebrate the fruits of our labors.

After months of hard work, our faith in God has given us the chance to start anew. Our first crops of corn, squash, and beans have been harvested, and William Bradford, our newly elected Governor, ordered a party of men to go out fowling to fetch birds back for the feast. There was also a good store of wild turkeys—large, strange-looking birds that are a common sight here.

We were about 50 in number and were joined by our new ally Massasoit and at least 90 of his people, who brought deer for the feast. We were all mesmerized by the sight of deer and birds turning on wooden spits over outdoor fires, transforming into succulent cooked meats.

We ate heartily and shared the best of what we had with Massasoit and his people. The feast lasted three days, and we played games. Everywhere around us looked as beautiful as God intended, the green leaves of summer turning brilliant yellow and red.

What began as a terrible year of struggle and sickness is ending in a spirit of gratitude to God.

The colony's future now seems more assured. We are less fearful of the Native people as some have now become our trusted allies. We give thanks for our good fortune.

> TRADITION has it that the first Thanksgiving took place in 1621, when the Plymouth settlers shared a meal celebrating the harvest with their Native allies. But it wasn't until 1789 that President George Washington officially named Thursday November 26 as a "Day of Publick Thanksgiving." The dates of Thanksgiving varied under subsequent presidents until Abraham Lincoln's famous 1863 proclamation that it should be held in November.

PILGRIM SETTLERS DEMAND MORE LAND!

By our investigative reporter, Looking Mouse Time When the Herring Run, 1623

RUNNERS HAVE noted that the English are now moving beyond the palisade that surrounds their town.

They have been in our country three years, and in spite of the agreement with Massasoit and the allied villages, they once again have not approached our leaders in regard to the use of more land. This land is still within the bounds of the Wampanoag Nation, and Massasoit was chosen to oversee that responsibility.

Runners observe each English family clearing new ground to plant more corn. The total area appears twice as large as that originally settled on.

> WILLIAM BRADFORD, originally from Yorkshire, England, was repeatedly elected Governor of the Plymouth colony between 1621 and 1657. An entry from his chronicle, dated 1623, shows the impact on the community made by offering families parcels of land to own. He writes: "The women now went willingly into the field, and took their little ones with them to set corn; which before would allege weakness and inability." Private land ownership as a form of individual incentive became a hallmark of immigrant culture, as distinct from the shared land ownership principles of Native peoples.

The sachems and elders agree this is a dangerous precedent. These English want more land now—and how much more in the future?

Another ship has already arrived, bringing even more people to settle here.

They have been informed as to which sachems are responsible for which lands, yet most disregard our laws and boundaries. Each day brings another intrusion for our people to contend with.

BIRTH OF BOSTON
PURITANS CREATE "CITY UPON A HILL"

By our newssheet writer in Boston
September 8, 1630

PURITAN elders declared yesterday that the Shawmut Peninsula will be called "Boston" in the future. The seat of government of the Massachusetts Bay Colony, which began two years ago, will also be in Boston.

It follows a meeting between John Winthrop, the colony's elected governor and clergyman William Blackstone, one of the first settlers to live in Trimount on the peninsula, so called because of its three "mountains." Blackstone recommended its spring waters.

Winthrop (pictured) left England earlier this year to lead ships across the Atlantic. Of the hundreds of passengers on board, many were Puritans seeking religious freedom, eager to start a new life in New England. They had prepared well, bringing many horses and cows with them.

The new governor, a member of the English upper classes, brought the royal charter of the Massachusetts Bay Company with him. However, the company's charter did not impose control from England—the colony would be effectively self-governing.

Arriving in Cape Ann, the passengers went ashore and picked fresh strawberries—a welcome change from shipboard life! Colonists had previously settled in the area, but dwellings had been abandoned after many had died in the harsh winter or were starving.

One early colonist was Roger Conant, who established Salem near the Native Naumkeag people. But Winthrop and the other Puritan leaders chose not to settle there, but to continue the search for their own Promised Land.

As Winthrop told his fellow Puritans: "We shall be as a City upon a Hill; the eyes of all people are upon us." After a temporary stay in Charlestown, Boston will be their permanent home.

Its name is said to have been chosen by Puritan clergyman Isaac Johnson, who once lived in the English town of Boston. The ship *Arbella*, which Winthrop sailed on, is said to be named for Johnson's wife Arabella.

Although Winthrop's Puritans got off to a better start than the Pilgrims ten years before, the colony has struggled with illness and tragedy in recent months, and dozens have died. The governor's own son Henry drowned in July.

The Massachuset and other Native peoples suffered in the great dying, their numbers

drastically reduced by disease. But Winthrop is taking few chances by spreading out settlements to make it difficult for potentially hostile groups to attack.

In time, Winthrop believes many more Puritans will flock to his "City upon a Hill" to build a godly community, and to prosper. The harbor at Boston is a natural wonder with potential to become a great center of trade.

ESTABLISHED in 1636, Harvard was created by the "Great and General Court of the Governor and Company of the Massachusetts Bay in New England." The college was named for clergyman John Harvard of Charlestown, an early benefactor who had emigrated to North America from England where he had studied at Cambridge University. In its early years, Harvard trained many Puritan ministers. An Indian College for Native Americans was also established at Harvard in 1655.

Martyrs' fight for religious freedom

QUAKER Mary Dyer was hanged yesterday after re-entering the Massachusetts Bay Colony against the orders of Puritan authorities, *writes our senior chronicler, June 2, 1660*. Claiming to be on a mission from God, she showed little emotion after being sentenced to death for her acts.

Last year she had resisted being banished from the state, but escaped hanging after her son pleaded with the authorities. Two fellow Quakers were not so fortunate—they were hanged on Boston Common for re-entering the colony. Although Dyer was spared the first time, she was told never to return—an order she has ignored.

In the early years of the colony, the Puritans often did not accept people whose beliefs differed from their own. They limited voting rights to male colonists who were church members.

Preacher Roger Williams was accused of "new and dangerous opinions" and was forced to flee the colony for present-day Rhode Island in 1636. He established a new colony where people were free to worship as they pleased.

Later, Anne Hutchinson defended her right, as a woman, to preach the Gospel. She clashed with John Winthrop, who had been re-elected governor and was outraged to learn of her controversial preaching in Boston.

Hutchinson was tried before Puritan elders, and sentenced to banishment. She sought sanctuary in present-day Rhode Island.

After moving further south, Hutchinson and many of her children were later massacred by a group of Siwanoy warriors during Kieft's War, a conflict between Dutch settlers and Native peoples.

Many believe Dyer and Hutchinson will one day be important symbols of religious freedom in America.

ENGLISH INTENSIFY EFFORTS TO CONVERT

THE ENGLISH came here so they could worship as they saw fit, unfettered by the powers in their home country. But once established, they immediately began efforts to force Wampanoag, Nipmuc, Narragansett, Pequot, and others from this land to follow their ways, *writes our investigative reporter Looking Mouse, Winter Moon, 1651.*

To the north, John Eliot preaches to all who will listen. To the south, Thomas Mayhew preaches on Noepe and Nantucket. Richard Bourne preaches from Manomet to Massipee, and throughout the Narrow Land.

Reports tell us Hiacoomes from Chappaquiddick was the first Wampanoag to convert in 1643. Many people have converted, but many others see this religion as the end of our ancient way of life. This has caused much strife and division in our communities.

Now Eliot has established a "Praying Town" at Natick, with many more planned. The goal is to make Indian people English. They must comply with the set regulations, or receive fines or punishment. This threatens not only our way of life, but our very lives. Yet many agree to live this way in order to live at all.

MANY MYTHS surround the arrival of the English settlers. One is that the Indians welcomed the Pilgrims with open arms. Another is the "peace treaty" of 1621. And everyone's heard of the First Thanksgiving! Another huge misunderstanding is the idea of 50 years of peace until King Philip's War in 1675.

If there were truly 50 years of peace, then why did the war take place?

Many things occurred that were not very peaceful. By the 1630s, the English settlers wanted more and more Wampanoag land. They forced Wampanoag and other tribal nations of the region to convert to Christianity. They created early reservations, or Indian districts, to move Native people off land that they wanted.

They developed laws that prevented Native people from following traditional ways. Native children were forcibly taken from their families and given to English families, who believed this was for their own good.

These are only some of the colonial practices used to dominate, control, or get rid of Native people. The Wampanoag and others negotiated, compromised, and tried to work with the English until they saw no alternative but war if they were going to save any of their lands and traditional ways.

All of the mythology of the English settlers and Indians being "friends" distorts, or hides, the true history. There was no 50 years of peace. This is why Native people today sometimes find conventional interpretations of history offensive.

TERRIBLE COST OF KING PHILIP'S WAR

By our war correspondent
August 13, 1676

KING PHILIP, a son of Wampanoag sachem Massasoit, was killed near the Pokanoket council seat yesterday, ending one of the bloodiest conflicts on New England soil. Metacom—who became known as "King Philip"—united many Indigenous peoples to defend their lands and traditional way of life against European settlers.

King Philip's War, which began over a year ago, has left thousands of people either dead or wounded. At one time, it looked as if the English would be driven out, after their towns were destroyed across the region. But colonial militias eventually defeated Native soldiers, burning their towns and villages.

Metacom's head will be impaled on a pike—to be displayed in Plymouth for 25 years. One hand will be sent to Boston, the other to England. His wife and son, along with the families of other Native people, are being sold into slavery. Lands held by those people who fought against the colonists will also be seized.

Ever since Massasoit's alliance with Plymouth Colony, there have been few openly violent clashes between Native Americans and European settlers in the area. But tensions have been rising ever since the settlers arrived.

Some blame Massasoit for allowing ancestral lands to be given away to colonists. They say King Philip realized what was happening and tried to curb their expansion. Others talk of a huge misunderstanding: Native Americans believed their lands were being offered "for use" to colonists; the colonists, on the other hand, thought they were selling "ownership."

The "Praying Towns" of John Eliot and other Puritan missionaries sought to extinguish Native American traditions and culture. Converted to Christianity, "praying Indians" have been expected to give up their ancient way of life. Hundreds of them have been interned in the war, their future uncertain. Not all Native peoples have sided with King Philip. Some fought alongside the English or stayed neutral.

John Sassamon, one of the first Wampanoag people to study at Harvard, was an interpreter to Metacom. He was found dead in suspicious circumstances last year, possibly for acting as an English informant. Did the controversial trial and execution of the Native Americans accused of his murder spark the conflict?

King Philip's death marks a turning point in the Native people's efforts to maintain their way of life in the face of colonial expansion.

COLLEGE STRUGGLES TO ATTRACT NATIVES, DISEASE TAKES ITS TOLL

THE ONLY Native student to graduate from the Harvard Indian College died yesterday, *writes our obituaries editor, 1666.*

Caleb Cheeshateaumuck lost his young life to consumption, a disease of the lungs that causes serious bleeding and difficulty with breathing. Caleb had become ill from his poor living conditions at the College.

The Indian College was established at Harvard in 1655 as a way for Harvard to continue receiving funding.

Its goal was effectively to turn Native youth into whites. However, in ten years, only five Native students have ever attended.

There were three Nipmuc men, brothers Benjamin and Eleazar Larnell, and James Printer; and two Wampanoag from Martha's Vineyard, Joel Hiacoomes and Caleb.

The Larnell brothers died from malnutrition and their living conditions. Meanwhile, Joel died in a shipwreck one month before graduation, and never received his degree.

The only living student, James Printer, whose Native name is Wowaus, works at the college's printing press as a printer. He has already helped produce more than 1,000 copies of the Eliot Bible, a translation of the Christian text into Wampanoag.

> The Harvard Indian College closed in 1693. Harvard eventually granted Joel Hiacoomes his degree in 2011.

WITCH-HUNT IN FULL SWING

By our religious affairs correspondent
October 29, 1692

SHOCKING events have taken place in Salem, where 20 men and women have been executed for witchcraft.

Despite professing their innocence, 19 have been hanged, and one man has been horribly crushed to death with stones. Only those who confessed have been spared.

Their accusers have included an enslaved woman called "Tituba" and children gripped by fits. Doctors have examined them but found nothing wrong.

In much of Europe, witchcraft is a heresy tried by the church, but English law considers it a crime to be tried in a court. The accused have been sent to the gallows based on little more than "spectral evidence"—the dreams and "visions" of the accusers.

Salem is not the only town in New England to be gripped by witchhunt

hysteria, but nowhere else have suspected witches been punished on such a terrible scale.

Many are suspicious of "spectral evidence," and hope that the people of Salem will come to their senses and recognize that innocent people are dying.

NO TAXATION WITHOUT REPRESENTATION

A BOSTON lawyer and pamphleteer is a leading critic of Britain's attempt to impose taxes on American colonists without their consent, *writes our civil rights editor, December 20, 1765*.

James Otis Jr. strongly opposes taxation without representation. He also denounces the Stamp Act, which imposes a tax on printed materials and which, he says, threatens to bring the justice system to a halt.

In his earlier pamphlet, *The Rights of the British Colonies Asserted and Proved*, he criticizes the British monarchy of George III: "that no parts of His Majesty's dominions can be taxed without their consent; that every part has a right to be represented—." His words are being taken up by patriots who want to unite Britain's 13 American colonies against these tax measures.

Britain is seeking to tax its American colonies to help pay for the recent French and Indian War. But colonists are angry about Britain's demands, having already provided militias to help Britain defeat France in the war, which took place in north eastern North America.

Patriots are saying the British government should heed the words of Otis, whose intellect and legal talent are respected by many. Otis argues that because the colonists do not have a representative in the British Parliament, the Parliament has no authority to tax them. His views are almost a declaration of independence.

Colonists are also unhappy about Britain's attempt to control trade in America. Boston merchants led the protests, objecting to a sugar tax by refusing to trade in luxury goods imported from Britain.

Along with Otis, other influential figures are starting to emerge from Massachusetts, including Samuel "Sam" Adams, son of a merchant and brewer, and John Hancock, another merchant.

IN 1757, during the French and Indian War, 800 Massachusetts militia helped defend Fort William Henry, a British garrison in upstate New York, attacked by French troops and their Native allies. The fort surrendered, but the British and colonists—including women and children—were killed. The battle was dramatized in *The Last of the Mohicans*, James Fenimore Cooper's classic novel published in 1826.

By our chief reporter
March 6, 1770

A BLOODY MASSACRE

THEY ARE CALLING it the "Boston Massacre." British soldiers fired on an angry mob yesterday, killing at least three colonists and injuring others. A 17-year-old boy died earlier today; a fifth person—a man—is said to be close to death.

Violence erupted in front of the Custom House after a young colonist was struck by a British officer. When a small group of soldiers came to help a colleague on guard duty, they were confronted by a mob.

The mob dared the soldiers to shoot, and in an instant, the men lay dead—Crispus Attucks, who was Nipmuc and Black, among them. It is unclear whether the soldiers' commanding officer, Captain Thomas Preston, ordered them to fire.

The Boston Massacre is certain to fan the flames of revolution across colonial America. Trouble has been brewing for some time. Boston-born Samuel Adams—said to be a founder of the Sons of Liberty patriot group—has been criticized for stirring up mob violence against British rule.

Adams rejects Britain's authority to impose taxes on its 13 American colonies and calls on them to unite in action. In Massachusetts, support is growing for Adams' style of leadership.

Citizens of Boston have also been angered by British troops, called "redcoats," parading through their streets. They see the troops' presence as an act of hostility by the British government.

As tensions between Britain and its colonists threaten to erupt into armed conflict, one Massachusetts lawyer is trying to uphold the law. John Adams, second cousin of Samuel Adams, opposes many of Britain's policies in America, but will later defend the British soldiers who carried out the Boston Massacre. He will maintain that the soldiers are entitled to a proper defense and that the men acted legally in the face of intimidation by a mob.

Enslaved woman wins her freedom

By our civil rights correspondent
November 5, 1766

JENNY SLEW is one of the first people held as a slave to be granted freedom through trial by jury. Boston-born lawyer Benjamin Kent represented Slew, who was kidnapped from her home in Ipswich and forced into servitude. Kent is said to be a member of the Sons of Liberty and friend of John Adams.

Slew, whose mother was a free white woman and father was of African descent, was awarded four pounds—the British unit of money—in damages. Legal experts say slavery in Massachusetts may die out if future court cases are successful.

Massachusetts has been involved in the slave trade since the early 17th century. It was even made legal for the children of enslaved people to be sold into slavery. Boston ships have been selling enslaved people to Rhode Island, Connecticut, and Virginia for decades. About 4,000 enslaved people reside in Massachusetts, though Boston's free African-American population is large.

Ports such as Boston and Salem have also grown wealthy from the trade—between North America, Britain, and Africa—which is built on slavery. Typically, the West Indies exports raw sugar or molasses to New England, where it is turned into rum. The rum is then shipped to Britain along with lumber and other items. Britain then transports textiles, rum, and manufactured goods to Africa to be traded for enslaved people destined for the West Indies, and the cycle starts again.

RECENT SCHOLARSHIP suggests that American slavery began in earliest colonial times, targeting people of the New England Indigenous Nations. The general perception has been that slavery was less common in an "enlightened" New England. However, throughout the 17th century, Native people comprised the vast majority of enslaved persons. Native slavery was an immediate and lucrative way to finance rebuilding "New England" after the devastation of King Philip's War. Thousands of Native people were shipped to the West Indies and Bermuda.

BOSTON HARBOR HOLDS PROTESTERS "TEA PARTY!"

By our politics editor
December 17, 1773

IN A DARING protest against British rule, a group of colonists dumped hundreds of chests full of British tea into Boston Harbor last night. Armed with axes, hatchets, and pistols, the patriots raided three ships anchored in the harbor—the *Dartmouth*, the *Eleanor*, and the *Beaver*.

The rebels, dressed as Native Americans to disguise themselves, opened the tea chests onboard and tossed their contents into the sea. None of the British sailors on the ships was injured.

Destruction of the tea is a direct challenge to Britain's authority. Patriots are angry at its government's attempt to control the tea trade in the American colonies by imposing import taxes on tea supplied by the British East India Company. This hated "tea tax" has become a symbol for both sides of Britain's right to govern.

John Adams, a moderate patriot who nevertheless supported the protest, declared the tea's destruction "so bold, so daring, so firm" that it must have "important consequences."

Earlier, the patriots told one of the ship owners to leave Boston with the hated tea cargo, but he refused, saying that to do so would bring about his ruin.

Matters were made worse when royal governor Thomas Hutchinson refused to let the ships leave without paying import duties. He is keen to make a stand against the Sons of Liberty patriot group, which he believes is masterminding the opposition.

Thousands of patriots gathered around Boston's Old South Meeting House, and Samuel Adams warned: "This meeting can do nothing more to save the country."

The "tea tax" is the last in a series of attempts by Britain to tax its American colonies. The Stamp Act of 1765 proved a spectacular failure, and had to be repealed.

Colonial resistance has turned into rebellion, though few are publicly calling for independence at this stage. Conflict with Britain looks unavoidable nevertheless. Some fear its government will punish colonists in Massachusetts by closing the port of Boston.

THE SHOT HEARD ROUND THE WORLD

By our war correspondent
April 20, 1775

THE FIRST SHOTS of the Revolutionary War were fired at Lexington and Concord yesterday. The battles marked the beginning of a historic struggle for independence from Britain by its American colonies.

In the early morning light, colonial militia dared to stand in the path of British soldiers on Lexington Common. The colonists slowed the redcoats' advance on nearby Concord, where the patriots' weapons and supplies were said to be stored.

Outnumbered by British soldiers, the small group of militiamen began to scatter. Suddenly, there was a shot and then both sides opened fire. The conflict claimed the lives of eight colonists, while British casualties were light. In the patriots' group was Prince Estabrook, an enslaved man, who was wounded in the battle, and has become the first African-American soldier to fight in the American Revolution.

Later, hundreds of colonists battled redcoats at the North Bridge at Concord, gaining the upper hand. As the British retreated from the town, they were ambushed. In total, 73 redcoats and 49 patriots were killed.

The colonists likely prevailed because they had been tipped off the night before the attack. Craftsman Paul Revere rode on horseback from Boston to Lexington to spread the word that

WOODEN "liberty poles" were symbols of freedom and independence during the American Revolution, often erected by the Sons of Liberty in town squares across Massachusetts. Boston's famous Liberty Tree—an elm tree near Boston Common—also served as a rallying point for patriots and a site of protest against British rule. It was later cut down by British soldiers and American colonists loyal to the British Crown.

the redcoats were coming. British troops detained him before he reached Concord, but he was eventually let go when the fighting began. With the help of fellow patriots, his "midnight ride" spread the word, and is certain to go into legend.

Armed conflict has looked unavoidable for some time. Many colonists regard the British monarchy and its government as tyrannical. The British regard many colonists as disloyal, while Massachusetts was recently declared to be in a state of rebellion.

Armed colonists have been called "traitors" by the British, whose General Thomas Gage has been ordered to use force to stop the colonial rebels from stockpiling weapons. The patriots have set up Minutemen companies, ready to march at a moment's warning.

Massachusetts and the other American colonies are now at war with Britain. If they win, Lexington and Concord will go down in history as the birthplace of American freedom.

British victory at Bunker Hill proves costly

BRITISH FORCES won the Revolutionary War's first major conflict yesterday, but their victory in the Battle of Bunker Hill, at Charlestown, has proven costly, *writes our war reporter, June 18, 1775.*

The battle left about one thousand British dead or wounded—more than double the number of American casualties—after the redcoats made several attacks.

Earlier, patriots had dug in on Breed's Hill, but after the British forces overwhelmed them, the men were forced to retreat to Cambridge on the other side of Bunker Hill. British military leaders knew they had to win the battle, as defeat could prove to be a decisive loss by the British Empire in America. But they failed to cut off the patriots' retreat, which would have delivered a devastating blow to colonial forces. The Americans showed a thirst for battle, but could not overcome the British, whose soldiers are among the best trained in the world.

The battle has confirmed the need for the Continental Army, created several days ago by the Continental Congress—a convention of delegates from the American colonies. George Washington of Virginia, who fought alongside the British in the French and Indian War, has been chosen to lead the newly created army, whose troops are mainly from New England. He is expected to assume command in Cambridge. His challenge will be to turn an inexperienced citizens' army into a formidable fighting force.

PATRIOTS WIN THE SIEGE OF BOSTON
STORM FOILS PLANNED BRITISH ATTACK, WASHINGTON SENSES VICTORY

THE SIEGE of Boston is over. A British fleet yesterday left Boston Harbor with thousands of troops aboard, the result of a stunning first military victory by George Washington's Continental Army, *writes our war correspondent, March 18, 1776.*

The British are withdrawing from the port and sailing away to the safe haven of Halifax in Nova Scotia. Also aboard the departing fleet are hundreds of families who have decided to stay loyal to the British Crown.

Colonial forces have besieged British-held Boston for months. A breakthrough came earlier this month when the Continental Army captured and fortified Dorchester Heights, which overlooks the port. Cannons were then set up within the fortifications. These powerful weapons were captured last year at Fort Ticonderoga and recently brought on sleds hundreds of miles by Henry Knox, Washington's artillery chief.

The British were reluctant to risk a battle that could prove even bloodier than Bunker Hill. They had hoped to use their ships in the harbor to attack the colonial forces' position, but around the time of their planned attack, a storm set in, and the assault had to be canceled.

The decision to evacuate the town brings to an end years of occupation by British soldiers. Living in tents on Boston Common, the soldiers' presence has angered many citizens, who say their liberties have been ignored.

Last night, jubilant patriots sang "Yankee Doodle" as a symbol of pride across the city—no longer a song used by British military officers to mock colonial "Yankees."

INDEPENDENCE DECLARED!

By our politics editor
July 5, 1776

HISTORY WAS made yesterday when the Continental Congress approved the Declaration of Independence from Britain. This momentous event marks the birth of an independent United States of America.

Massachusetts was one of 12 American colonies to approve the declaration in Philadelphia. Only New York declined to vote. The pro-independence delegation from Massachusetts included lawyer John Adams, second cousin Samuel Adams, lawyer Robert Treat Paine, and Elbridge Gerry, a member of a wealthy merchant family. Businessman John Hancock served as president of the Congress.

Britain is certain to view this as an act of treason. As a result, the names of these "Founding Fathers" will be kept secret for the time being.

After months of soul-searching, the colonies have finally united against Britain. Rejecting its government's attempts to tax them, the colonies have come to regard the Revolutionary War as a struggle for liberty and freedom.

The declaration, whose principal author is Thomas Jefferson of Virginia, has been highly praised.

One passage reads: "We hold these truths to be self-evident, that all men are created equal, that they are endowed by their Creator with certain unalienable rights, that among these are life, liberty, and the pursuit of happiness." But Anti-slavery language has been removed—to the relief of some delegates, mainly from the South.

The declaration also makes the case against King George III and his "absolute tyranny," over the American colonies. "He has abdicated government here, by declaring us out of his protection, and waging war against us." John Adams predicts the declaration will forever be celebrated in America.

THE DECLARATION of Independence claims that "all men are created equal." It expounds on the harmful actions of the King, and details the reasons for a formal separation from Britain. In one seldom-cited passage, Indigenous people are not considered equal, but as violent savages: "He (the King) has excited domestic insurrections amongst us, and has endeavored to bring on the inhabitants of our frontiers, the merciless Indian savages, whose known rule of warfare is an undistinguished destruction of all ages, sexes, and conditions."

ALL MEN ARE BORN FREE AND EQUAL
MASSACHUSETTS CONSTITUTION WILL BE USED TO END SLAVERY IN THE STATE

By our civil rights editor
October 25, 1780

THE MASSACHUSETTS Constitution came into effect today, declaring that all men are born "free and equal." Many believe the new constitution effectively abolishes slavery, making it illegal. But women still do not have the right to vote.

The Revolutionary War continues to grind on, but after the Declaration of Independence in 1776 and the creation of the United States, the American colonies set about writing their own constitutions as free and independent states.

The Massachusetts Constitution is the basic governing document of the Commonwealth of Massachusetts. This new state replaces the Province of Massachusetts Bay, a royal colony formed nearly a century ago.

The old province included the Massachusetts Bay Colony and Plymouth Colony from the time of the Puritans and Pilgrims. Maine will remain part of Massachusetts, at least for the time being.

The constitution's principal author has been Massachusetts lawyer and patriot John Adams, who was a signer of the U.S. Declaration of Independence.

THE Massachusetts State House in Boston was completed in 1798 and has served as the seat of state government ever since. Designed by Charles Bulfinch, the state capitol building was constructed to take over from the Old State House, the scene of the Boston Massacre. Later, its dome will be gilded in gold leaf. A "Sacred Cod"—a wood-crafted symbol of the fishing industry—hung in the Old State House and today one hangs over the House of Representatives chamber in the "new" State House. In 1933, Massachusetts politicians were sent reeling after the theft of the Sacred Cod. Harvard students were suspected of being behind the prank, and it was eventually returned.

He built a reputation for respect for the law when he defended British soldiers' role in the Boston Massacre.

The Massachusetts Constitution was approved in June after a special convention was called, attended by representatives from towns across Massachusetts. The constitution states that under a "social compact" citizens agree to be governed by laws designed for the "common good."

The Commonwealth, it says, is "a free, sovereign, and independent state," with three branches of government.

They include a state governor, independent judiciary, and state legislature elected by the people, called the General Court of Massachusetts. It also officially recognizes Harvard as a university.

Legal experts are predicting that a court battle over the future of slavery in the state will intensify. Making use of the constitution, enslaved people are expected to bring legal actions to win their freedom. But some owners are likely to try and get around the law by keeping slaves as indentured servants.

BRAVE BID TO BEAT SMALLPOX

ABIGAIL ADAMS yesterday struck a courageous blow against the smallpox that is ravaging the Boston area, *writes our medical correspondent, July 13, 1776.*

While her husband John Adams campaigned for the Declaration of Independence in Philadelphia, Abigail Adams prepared her children for inoculation against deadly, disfiguring smallpox.

She brought her family from their Braintree farm into disease-ridden Boston, where she and her children were inoculated by Dr. Thomas Bulfinch, an expert.

Small amounts of smallpox-infected tissue were introduced into cuts made in the healthy children's arms. The hope is that the young patients will develop only minor cases of smallpox from this procedure. Then they will be immune from catching a more serious or deadly case of the disease later.

In previous attempts, it worked in some, but others suffered days of delirium and fever. And often the inoculation must be repeated.

The patients can take weeks to recover, but they will never again fear this disease—they will be immune for the rest of their lives. Although Adams and her children are not the first to be inoculated, their bravery will set an example.

SMALLPOX and other diseases seriously impacted the Native people in New England. There was an epidemic in every decade throughout the 17th century that took even further tolls on the populations of the Indigenous nations. In the 18th century, two thirds of the Nantucket Wampanoag people died after smallpox inoculation. Entire communities were wiped out, as were generations of ancestral knowledge about oral histories, relations with the Earth, and many cultural and spiritual traditions.

U.S. Constitution inspired by Adams' state model

GOVERNMENT UNDER the U.S. Constitution began today. Politicians representing Massachusetts have played a major role in establishing the U.S. Constitution, *writes our civil rights correspondent, March 4, 1789.*

The U.S. Constitution forms the body of laws governing the newly independent United States of America. The document strengthens the national government, which is now made up of the legislative branch, consisting of the U.S. Congress; the executive branch, including the president; and the judicial branch, consisting of the Supreme Court and other federal courts.

It has been partly modeled on the Massachusetts Constitution, though it permits slavery.

Getting approval for the new Constitution was no small feat. Anti-federalists feared that the Constitution would over-centralize government and restrict individual liberties. They demanded changes and a Bill of Rights to guarantee personal freedoms. Federalists, on the other hand, argued that states should accept the proposed Constitution without further changes.

When these opposing views clashed in Massachusetts, an agreement—known as the Massachusetts Compromise—was brokered by two famous local statesmen, John Hancock and Samuel Adams. Under it, Massachusetts ratified the Constitution, becoming the sixth U.S. state, while also proposing future amendments, including a Bill of Rights. The Massachusetts Compromise was used as a model by other states to reach similar agreements. Without it, the U.S. Constitution may never have been ratified at all.

The U.S. Constitution will be formally enacted next month alongside George Washington's inauguration as the first U.S. President.

JOHN ADAMS WINS PRESIDENTIAL RACE

By our politics editor
February 8, 1797

TODAY is a proud day for the people of Massachusetts. Braintree-born John Adams, a signer of the Declaration of Independence, has at last been elected as the second U.S. President. He succeeds George Washington, after serving as his Vice President.

In the first contested American presidential election, Adams' main rival was Thomas Jefferson, who becomes the next Vice President. Presidential electors were appointed by state legislatures or chosen by popular vote. Adams received 71 electoral votes, narrowly beating Jefferson's 68, to win the presidency.

As the nation's seat of government takes shape in Washington, DC, the president will reside in a new "Presidential Mansion" currently under construction, that some are already calling the "White House."

Adams is a distinguished statesman, lawyer, and principal author of the Massachusetts state constitution, upon which the U.S. Constitution has been partly modeled.

During the American Revolution, Adams served as a Massachusetts delegate at the Continental Congress. Later, as a diplomat in Europe, Adams helped negotiate a peace treaty with Britain that recognized American independence.

SECOND U.S. President John Adams and third U.S. President Thomas Jefferson died within hours of each other on Independence Day, 1826. The political rivals became friends in later years, writing to each other. Their letters—a look inside the minds of the Founding Fathers—were published for all to enjoy. Adams, aged 90, uttered his last words: "Thomas Jefferson still survives." Little did he know that Jefferson, aged 83, had died several hours earlier.

A close adviser to Adams is his wife Abigail, who, despite being deprived of a formal education, is known for her intellectual prowess and insights on politics and women's rights. Their son, John Quincy Adams, has been appointed a U.S. ambassador.

As a young nation, America is already showing itself determined to follow its own course. Although France helped it defeat Britain, the U.S. wants to stay "neutral" in France's latest war with Britain.

Adams must deal with growing tensions between the U.S. and France, which is in the midst of its own revolution, especially as French privateers have started seizing ships to halt American trade with Britain.

SPRINGFIELD ARMORY COMES OF AGE

By our defense correspondent
February 18, 1815

THE U.S. ARMORY at Springfield, Massachusetts, has helped restore America's honor after the nation's latest conflict with Britain. The War of 1812 has formally ended. To the relief of citizens on both sides, a treaty has settled the northeastern border between America and British-controlled Canada.

The Springfield armory played an important role as a big provider of weapons to American forces. It made nearly 10,000 muskets last year.

They say the Springfield armory has finally come of age after a slow start. In 1795, as the nation's first government-run armory, 40 workers were expected to produce just 245 muskets in its first year of operation.

America held its own against a world power, but experts warn that without strong defenses in the future, the nation will struggle to secure its independence and freedoms.

They predict Springfield muskets will one day be famous as the factory builds a reputation for clever engineering and manufacturing.

The armory was chosen by George Washington to serve as the main weapons arsenal during the Revolutionary War.

Toward the end of the last century, it looked as if the French might invade the U.S. even though they had previously helped the young nation defeat the British in the Revolutionary War. America decided to prepare for possible conflict by building up its navy and rearming.

In 1798, Eli Whitney, who grew up on a farm in Massachusetts, won a contract to produce 10,000 muskets. He has been called a pioneer of the machine age after his factory helped to develop "interchangeable parts" to mass-produce weapons.

Earlier, Whitney was granted a patent after inventing the cotton gin, a device to remove seeds from cotton. The "gin"—short for "engine"—has boosted the economy of southern slave-owning states, and led some to criticize the invention for reviving slave plantations.

AMERICANS MOURN DEATH OF ABOLITIONIST

PAUL CUFFE, WHO HAS DIED AGED 58, CROSSED RACIAL AND CULTURAL DIVIDES

By our obituaries editor
October 22, 1817

RENOWNED shipowner, merchant and political campaigner Paul Cuffe died last month in the town of Westport, Massachusetts, marking the end of a remarkable life. A devout, hard-working sailor and entrepreneur, Cuffe was a self-made man, rising to become one of the wealthiest men of mixed race in America.

Cuffe was born on January 17, 1759 to Cuffe Slocum, a freed slave and skilful carpenter, and Ruth Moses, from the Wampanoag tribe of Aquinnah on the island of Martha's Vineyard. After taking his father's first name as his surname following his father's

death in 1772, Cuffe became a seaman, serving on whaling ships and then, during the Revolutionary War, as a privateer smuggling supplies through the British blockades. In 1783, he married Alice Pequit, a member of the Pequot tribe of Connecticut with whom he had seven children.

After the war, Cuffe opened a shipyard with his brother-in-law and became a successful merchant and farm owner. A committed Quaker, Cuffe combined hard work and resourcefulness with a political conscience: Paul and his brother John refused to pay their taxes in the 1770s on the basis that, despite being free men, they were denied the right to vote and briefly jailed. However, their taxes were reduced following the dispute.

As his wealth and influence grew, Cuffe became a leading voice in the abolitionist and humanitarian movements to resettle freed slaves in Sierra Leone, and he sailed to Britain and West Africa to advance this cause. He also did much to help the poor at home, including establishing a smallpox hospital and a racially integrated school.

In 1812, after Cuffe's cargo was

seized on charges that it had broken an embargo, he traveled to Washington, D.C. to meet President Madison, who ordered its release. Cuffe is thought to be the first free black American to have been received by a sitting president at the White House.

The respect and affection widely felt for Cuffe is summarized by his friend Reverend Peter Williams Jr.: "Such was his reputation for wisdom and integrity, that his neighbors always consulted him in all their important concerns; and, oh! what honor to the son of an African slave, the most respectable men in Great Britain and America were not ashamed to seek him for counsel and advice!"

NEW DAWN OF INDUSTRY

By our industry correspondent
March 1, 1826

THE MILL TOWN of Lowell in Massachusetts has been created in honor of Francis Cabot Lowell, a pioneer of America's Industrial Revolution. His cotton mill in Waltham was the first in the U.S. to turn raw cotton into finished cloth, all under one roof.

Created by a Boston association of investors, a group eager to exploit recent advances in technology, Lowell will serve as a model for the new industrial age. The new town will be a center for textile mills and factories and will be powered by an ambitious canal system. The mills will weave cotton picked by slaves in southern states and transported to the North.

Much of Massachusetts has become a hotbed of technology. The state is at the forefront of the Industrial Revolution and is fast becoming the workshop of America. Factories are springing up everywhere, producing tools and paper as well as wool and cotton textiles.

A chain bridge at Newburyport is said to be the first suspension bridge in the U.S. And the Middlesex Canal is one of the first engineering projects of its kind. Completed in 1803, it connects the Merrimack River to Boston, opening up new opportunities. In Woburn, the canal allows vessels to deliver bark to tanneries, which create dye from the bark and use it to color leather. As a result, the town's shoemaking and leather businesses are booming.

Despite technological advances, many factories still rely on child labor to operate machinery. The children are often treated harshly, their safety neglected.

There are few calls to ban child labor, but campaigners want the state to limit children's daily working hours and require them to attend school for some months of the year.

Under Francis Cabot Lowell's system, young women, or "Mill Girls," carry out the work, though they are paid less than men, and children are not employed.

THE PLYMOUTH Cordage Company, founded in 1824, became one of the largest producers of rope and twine in the world. In the late 19th century, its workforce got a significant boost from a new wave of immigrants from Italy, Portugal, and Alsace-Lorraine. The company specialized in ship rigging—ropes used to hold up and control the sails—and made the rope used on the USS *Constitution*. To make rope, workers put fibers around their waists and walked backward down the 90-foot-long rope walk as they twisted the fibers. The company was the largest employer in Plymouth for more than 100 years. Another Massachusetts industrial success story is Crane Currency, a 200-year-old papermaking company from Dalton which in 1879 won the contract to make the paper used for U.S. banknotes.

SON FOLLOWS FATHER TO PRESIDENCY

JOHN QUINCY ADAMS—lawyer, diplomat, and eldest son of second U.S. President John Adams—became the sixth U.S. President today, *writes our politics editor, February 9, 1825*.

He was chosen by the U.S. House of Representatives after all four presidential candidates failed to win an electoral majority.

Like his father, John Quincy Adams was born in Braintree and was named for his great-grand-father John Quincy—for whom the town of Quincy was named.

Before his presidency, he spent many years as a diplomat in Europe and helped negotiate an end to the War of 1812. As secretary of state, Adams negotiated the Adams-Onís Treaty, in which Spain ceded Florida to the U.S. He also represented the state of Massachusetts, serving in both the U.S. Senate and the House of Representatives.

One story—possibly untrue—claims the President will be keeping an alligator in the White House. Supposedly, it was a gift from the Marquis de Lafayette of France, a hero of the American Revolution who has been visiting the U.S.

John Adams and John Quincy Adams are the first father-and-son duo to become U.S. presidents.

PREACHER LEADS MASHPEE REVOLT

MASHPEE Wampanoag in Cape Cod have won a degree of self-rule following the Mashpee Revolt, *writes our civil rights correspondent, March 31, 1834.*

The Mashpees became unhappy about the way the state was running their reservation after ending self-government. They were also angry at the theft of wood from their forests by white men.

Led by William Apess, a Pequot preacher who moved to Massachusetts, the group informed the state that they would rule themselves from now on and that white men could no longer take wood without their permission.

The Massachusetts authorities were alarmed at first, but then agreed to return a degree of self-government.

It was Mashpee Wampanoag whalers who planned, wrote, and executed the laws that resulted in self-government. They claim to have been inspired by the freedom of whales.

Despite the victory, there are lingering fears the state will intervene to break up the Mashpee tribal lands.

As elsewhere in America, Wampanoag and other Native people in Massachusetts suffer discrimination and the denial of basic rights.

DEATH OF A NATIONAL FOLK HERO

By our agriculture correspondent
March 23, 1845

THE DEATH of John Chapman, better known as folk hero "Johnny Appleseed," was confirmed yesterday. Born and raised in Leominster, he left Massachusetts for the Midwest, where American and European settlers were starting farms. He is said to have carried a bag of apple seeds on his travels and became famous for planting trees across the Midwest.

Countless stories exist about the life of Johnny Appleseed, who has come to symbolize the pioneering spirit of America's expanding frontier. He often walked miles every day, sleeping outdoors.

He was also known for treating animals with kindness. One story goes that while lying by his cozy campfire, he noticed that mosquitoes were getting burned in the blaze. The storyteller recounts: "Johnny, who wore on his head a tin utensil which answered both as a cap and a mush pot, filled it with water and quenched the fire, and afterwards remarked, 'God forbid that I should build a fire for my comfort, that should be the means of destroying any of His creatures.'"

There are few details about his early life, though it is known that his mother died when he was young. He planted his first apple orchards in Pennsylvania before traveling to Ohio. There, he used cider apples to make an alcoholic beverage that Midwestern pioneers could consume when there was limited access to clean drinking water.

A follower of mystic Emanuel Swedenborg, Johnny Appleseed often told stories and spread his faith to children and adults.

Chapman died in Indiana last week, aged about 70. A notice of his death said he was well known for his eccentricity and wearing "strange garb." The notice stated: "He is supposed to have considerable property, yet denied himself almost the common necessities of life. In the most

LONG before the arrival of Europeans, Wampanoag people ate wild cranberries that grew naturally in bogs across southeastern Massachusetts, and valued their medicinal qualities. In 1816, Henry Hall, a Revolutionary War veteran from the town of Dennis, began commercial cultivation after discovering cranberries grew better when sand had blown over them. Others adopted his technique, and the industry boomed. Cranberry bogs still nestle among the region's towns and villages.

inclement weather he might be seen barefooted and almost naked except when he chanced to pick up articles of old clothing." Despite his devotion to poverty, John Chapman leaves an estate of more than a thousand acres of orchards to his sister.

DOUGLASS EXPOSES EVILS OF SLAVERY

By our civil rights correspondent
May 2, 1845

FREDERICK DOUGLASS has been hailed a new national leader of the abolitionists' anti-slavery movement after his autobiography was published yesterday.

Narrative of the Life of Frederick Douglass, an American Slave describes his earlier years as an enslaved man and his struggle for freedom. He wrote the book in the town of Lynn, after he became a free man. The work is predicted to become an instant bestseller, adding momentum to the campaign to end slavery across America.

The book describes the evils of slavery in chilling detail. But some whites question his authorship, saying a slave is incapable of writing such a work.

In the book, Douglass recounts his early life, years in which he saw an aunt whipped and enslaved people punished by their masters, even for telling the truth. Later, one particularly cruel owner regularly whipped Douglass, working and beating him to exhaustion, until Douglass collapsed one day while working in the fields.

Somehow, Douglass learned to write, and read everything he could to educate himself.

Eventually, he escaped to the North, reaching New Bedford, where he lived for a time. The whaling port town has become an important stop on the Underground Railroad—the network of secret routes and safe houses used by southern slaves to escape to northern free states and Canada. Many fugitive slaves have found places in whaling crews.

For years now, abolitionists have been drawn to Massachusetts. The 1780 Massachusetts Constitution, drafted primarily by John Adams, second U.S. President, effectively abolished slavery in the state. Using the state constitution, enslaved people won their freedom in a series of court cases, including Elizabeth Freeman and Quock Walker. In Boston's Beacon Hill, free African-Americans and escaped slaves have helped to make the state a center of the national anti-slavery movement.

Elsewhere, African-American campaigner Sojourner Truth, who was born into slavery, joined a community in Northampton, while John Brown, a leading white abolitionist, moved to Springfield.

In 1831, William Lloyd Garrison published *The Liberator,* a Boston newspaper that called for the immediate emancipation of all slaves

in the U.S. A white man born in Newburyport, Garrison is a cofounder of the American Anti-Slavery Society and an early advocate for women's right to vote, inspiring many African-Americans—including Frederick Douglass—to make their voices heard.

EDUCATION CHAMPION TAKES SEAT

BETWEEN 1845–1849 famine struck Ireland after the country's potato crop was blighted. Thousands of starving Irish-Catholic families fled to America. The Irish had been coming to Massachusetts for decades to work, but not in such great numbers. Many settled in cities such as Boston, where they faced anti-Catholic prejudice and a life of poverty. A Boston memorial to the Great Famine, unveiled in 1998, has since caused controversy on both sides of the Atlantic.

HORACE MANN, the Franklin-born educational reformer, yesterday began a new chapter in his remarkable career—as a Member of the U.S. House of Representatives from Massachusetts. He plans to make his first congressional speech on the evils of slavery, *writes our education correspondent, April 4, 1848.*

Mann is best known for championing public education. It has been said no one has done more to establish that, in a democratic society, education should be free and universal, and promote civic virtue.

As Secretary of the Massachusetts Board of Education, he has won support for building public schools. Since then, many U.S. states have adopted a version of the education system he has pioneered in Massachusetts.

Mann strongly believes that education should be provided by well-trained, professional teachers. To this end, he devised a "normal" school system for the training of professional teachers in Bridgewater and other centers in Massachusetts. He believes that women are particularly well suited to becoming teachers.

Mann, whose father was a farmer, grew up facing poverty and hardship. He had little schooling as a boy but made use of Franklin Public Library, one of America's first public lending libraries. Aged 20, he gained admission to Brown University. He later served in the Massachusetts legislature after choosing law as a career.

THE STRUGGLE FOR WOMEN'S RIGHTS

By our civil rights editor
October 25, 1850

THE first annual National Women's Rights Convention ended in triumph yesterday. At the historic gathering in Worcester, delegates from 11 U.S. states heard speeches on women's right to vote as well as their right to equal wages and to own property.

Both women and men attended the two-day convention at Brinley Hall, which attracted activists from as far away as the new U.S. state of California.

The press, sensing a good story, were not always kind to the participants. One newspaper called them a "motley mingling." Lucy Stone (right), of West Brookfield—the first woman from Massachusetts to earn a college degree—was one of the main organizers. She called for women to have the right to vote

and to own property. Ernestine Rose, who fled Poland for America, said: "We have heard a great deal of our Pilgrim Fathers ... but who has heard of the Pilgrim Mothers?"

Abby Kelley Foster urged listeners not to argue over women's rights but to seize them, "as did our fathers against King George III." Sojourner Truth, the abolitionist born into slavery, gave a rousing speech on women's rights.

Elizabeth Cady Stanton, a leader in the women's rights movement, was unable to attend due to her pregnancy, but sent a letter of support: "The earth has never yet seen a truly great and virtuous nation, for woman has never yet stood the equal with man."

Others who attended were abolitionists Frederick Douglass and William Lloyd Garrison. Nantucket-born Lucretia Mott, who had helped to organize the Seneca Falls Convention of 1848, the first regional women's rights convention, also attended.

The gathering in Worcester is surely not the last: women are finding their voice, and plan to hold another convention next year.

EARLE REPORT SAYS INDIANS NOT SUITABLE AS CITIZENS

THE LATEST count of the Indians of Massachusetts has just been released. Commissioner John Milton Earle compiled the census and presented a report to the Governor's Council, *writes our staff reporter, Josiah Neesmuhshoonash, April 15, 1861.*

Responsibility for Indian tribes rests with the state. That means their numbers must be recorded, along with their social and living conditions. White overseers of Indian lands often allow non-Indians to graze sheep, cut from woodlots, or even build homes on Indian lands. However, Indian people say they want their allotted lands protected, allowing them to farm, hunt, and fish as they always have: "We still know the forests and the ancient roads and take heart in our remaining communities living throughout our old homelands," said a representative.

The report details 1,126 people

in 291 families, including each person's name, age, tribe, gender, occupation, place of residence, number of livestock, and amount of land owned.

However, those who roam from place to place, following old seasonal moves, do not get included in the count. The officials who compile the report are also free to decide who is Indian, judging a person's looks or skin color, rather than studying their family information or kinship.

The purpose of the report was to decide whether Indian people are ready to be granted full citizenship, giving them the same legal status as whites.

Earle concludes that Indians are not ready. "The disabilities under which we have placed them ... have perpetuated their unfitness to bear the burdens of citizenship. The history of all conquered ... races ... illustrates the impossibility of elevating such races. ..."

COMMERCIAL whaling in Massachusetts dates back to the 17th century, though Native Americans hunted whales long before and were in much demand by sea captains for their skills and expertise. As the industry flourished, immigrants from the Azores and Cape Verde settled in New Bedford. The hunt for whales was brilliantly captured in Herman Melville's classic 1851 novel *Moby Dick; or, The Whale*, with early scenes set in New Bedford and Nantucket.

BATTLE FOR GLORY

By our war reporter
July 19, 1863

AFRICAN-AMERICAN soldiers of the 54th Massachusetts Volunteer Infantry Regiment yesterday mounted an attack on Confederate-held Fort Wagner in the Civil War. Many were killed or wounded in the battle, but their bravery will live on forever.

The men showed no outward signs of fear as, along with other Union troops, they stormed the South Carolina fort under heavy fire. Robert Gould Shaw, their white commanding officer and son of Boston abolitionists, was killed atop the fort.

One of the bloodiest wars in U.S. history began more than two years ago after 11 southern states broke away from the Union. They feared that slavery, on which their farming economy has been built, would be banned under President Abraham Lincoln.

When Lincoln issued the Emancipation Proclamation in January—declaring that all slaves in rebel states were free—he made it possible for free men of color and newly liberated slaves to enlist in the Union Army.

The 54th and 55th Massachusetts Volunteers are among the first regiments of armed African-Americans to be organized by the northern states to fight in the war. Leading abolitionist and orator Frederick Douglass is serving as a recruiter for the Union Army's African-American units and has issued an appeal: "Men of Color, To Arms!"

The courage of the 54th is certain to inspire other African-Americans to enlist. According to eyewitnesses, Sergeant William Harvey Carney grabbed the U.S. flag after the flag bearer fell, bravely carrying it to the enemy. Despite the bloodshed yesterday, Fort Wagner remains in Confederate hands. Some think Carney's heroism should be recognized with the Medal of Honor.

Massachusetts—a center of the anti-slavery movement—strongly supports the Union cause. This "most Yankee of Yankee states" is expected to supply at least 150,000 soldiers and sailors to the war effort.

LUTHER BURBANK, the 13th child of his parents, grew up on a Massachusetts farm and became an expert in agricultural science. In 1872, he developed a new blight-resistant potato, helping avoid a repeat of the terrible effects of the Great Famine in Ireland. Burbank also developed many varieties of fruits, flowers, and other plants, including a spineless cactus. A variety of his "Burbank potato" is today among America's most cultivated crops.

Union victory ends slavery, but fight goes on and on

RECONSTRUCTION is seeking to transform America after the Union victory in the Civil War brought an end to slavery, *writes our politics editor, February 3, 1870.* Defeated Confederate states have been placed under U.S. military control, and millions of newly freed African-Americans are being promised basic human rights.

Southern "slave" states are being readmitted to the Union after consenting to the 13th, 14th and 15th Amendments to the U.S. Constitution. Taken together, they abolish slavery, provide citizens equal protection under the law, and give adult males the vote, whatever their "race, color, or previous condition of servitude."

It is a triumph for campaigners such as Charles Sumner (pictured below), a U.S. Senator from Massachusetts. Before the war, Sumner became famous for making an anti-slavery speech that led a pro-slavery congressman to beat him until he was unconscious.

Tragically, U.S. President Abraham Lincoln was assassinated, and did not live to see the results of Reconstruction.

Not all Massachusetts abolitionists agree on where the movement goes from here. With the battle for emancipation finally won, William Lloyd Garrison wants to disband the American Anti-Slavery Society he cofounded. For others, the struggle goes on. The vote has been extended to newly freed men, but not to women. In Massachusetts, segregated schools were banned in 1855, but many remain white or African-American.

At a Boston meeting, leading abolitionist Frederick Douglass previously warned of a "malignant spirit" in the pro-slavery South that will attempt to reverse gains made by the Union victory.

NEW AGE OF COMMUNICATIONS
TELEPHONE MAY SURPASS POPULARITY OF THE TELEGRAPH

By our technology editor
March 11, 1876

A Boston professor has invented the first practical telephone that promises to revolutionize communications in America and the rest of the world. Alexander Graham Bell made the historic breakthrough yesterday: he shouted into a mouthpiece in his Boston laboratory and successfully spoke to Thomas Watson on the receiving end of a telephone in a different room. Bell reportedly said: "Mr. Watson, come here—I want to see you," and to his delight, Watson came in and declared he had heard and understood what was said, repeating the words back to the professor.

The Scottish-born inventor has succeeded in electrically transmitting the human voice by wire. His telephone offers the prospect of people in different places having conversations with each other, perhaps even over long distances.

The mechanics of speech and sound have dominated Bell's education and upbringing. Bell developed a "finger language" to "talk" to his mother, who lost her hearing. His father was a celebrated teacher of elocution, or speech, in Edinburgh, Scotland. Today, Alexander Graham Bell describes himself as "a teacher of the deaf," and has trained instructors at the Boston School for Deaf Mutes. He went on to repeat the program at schools for the deaf in Northampton and Hartford, Connecticut.

Bell's invention is not the only big advance in communications to come out of Massachusetts. Charlestown-born Samuel Morse helped to develop the electric telegraph that spans America today, sending messages in Morse code. One day, Bell's invention may surpass the popularity of the telegraph.

Bell has received some financial support for his telephone experiments from a Boston lawyer as well as a Salem businessman, whose deaf son is Bell's student. The professor has also filed a patent to gain exclusive rights to

his invention and prevent others from copying it. For now, he appears to have beaten inventor Elisha Gray of Ohio, a major rival.

Experts predict that Bell's backers will naturally want to promote his invention by quickly establishing telephone companies.

BARTON FOUNDS AMERICAN RED CROSS

CLARA BARTON, who was born in North Oxford and became a Civil War nurse, has founded the American Red Cross, *writes our war correspondent, May 21, 1881.*

After spending time caring for a Massachusetts militia regiment at the start of the Civil War, the former teacher began collecting medical supplies, food, and clothing to aid Union soldiers. The supplies were not always available—at the Battle of Antietam, she had to resort to corn husks in place of bandages. Barton became known as the "Angel of the Battlefield."

After the war, Barton ran the Missing Soldiers Office, which assisted families looking for relatives killed or missing in action. She met Susan B. Anthony and Frederick Douglass and remains a supporter of women's suffrage and civil rights.

On a trip to Europe, she met leaders of the Red Cross in Geneva, Switzerland, and used the expertise she gained in the Civil War to help the humanitarian effort during the Franco-Prussian War.

The U.S. is understood to be ready to join a dozen or more European countries to honor the Red Cross flag—a symbol of neutrality of the armed forces'

medical services and civilian volunteers who treat the wounded.

Barton has succeeded in gaining U.S. support after pledging that the new American Red Cross will respond to wars and other crises.

AMERICA'S first subway system got rolling in Boston in 1897. The first "Big Dig" was designed to tackle urban traffic jams. Passengers rode in an open trolley car along a "subway" passage just six tenths of a mile long. Despite its short length, the subway marked a new era in mass transit in the U.S.

TAKE AIM FOR THE BASKET!

SPRINGFIELD TEACHER CREATES POPULAR NEW GAME

By our sports reporter
December 31, 1891

TO KEEP Springfield students active in winter, physical education teacher James Naismith has invented a new game called basketball—and its popularity is already spreading.

The game is thrilling students at the International YMCA Training School, where they are required to throw a large ball into peach baskets suspended from a balcony in the gym.

Naismith was ordered by the school to create an indoor game that was not too rough, but would provide an "athletic distraction" during the harsh winter months. He studied other popular sports and decided that a big soft ball was safest indoors. He sought to reduce body contact by placing the goal high above the players' heads.

Naismith described the origin of the first game in a handwritten report: "When Mr. Stubbins brought up the peach baskets to the gym, I secured them on the inside of the railing of the gallery ... I then put up the 13 rules on the bulletin board just behind the instructor's platform, secured a soccer ball, and awaited the arrival of the class. The class did not show much enthusiasm, but followed my lead."

The first game was not a success: the students began tackling, kicking, and punching, and it ended in a free-for-all.

Naismith is refining the game to make it cleaner by stopping tackling. He has named his new game "Basket Ball."

The game has already taken off and expert commentators believe it is sure to become one of the world's most popular sports.

DEAF-BLIND STUDENT EARNS COLLEGE DEGREE

By our education editor
June 29, 1904

A 24-YEAR-OLD student in Massachusetts yesterday became one of the first deaf-blind people to earn a college degree. Helen Keller, who lost her sight and hearing as a result of a childhood illness, graduated from the prestigious Radcliffe women's college in Cambridge.

Her remarkable achievement follows the publication of her autobiography, *The Story of My Life*, which tells of how, with the help of her teacher and companion, Anne Sullivan, she learned to read, write, and speak.

Keller (on the left) dedicated the book to Alexander Graham Bell, "who has taught the deaf to speak and enabled the listening

ear to hear speech from the Atlantic to the Rockies." She describes how Sullivan, who was born in Feeding Hills, Agawam, Massachusetts and has experienced periods of blindness herself, came to her after Bell recommended the

school that Sullivan had attended.

Sullivan's patient teaching helped Keller escape from the isolation of being unable to hear or see, which left her "at sea in a dense fog."

When Sullivan first met Keller, she found a little girl trapped in her own dark, silent world. But a

breakthrough came when she ran cool water over one of Keller's hands, spelling out the word "w-a-t-e-r" on her other hand with her fingers. Keller later explained: "The mystery of language was revealed to me."

Keller attended the Perkins School for the Blind—the same school that Sullivan had graduated from—and the Horace Mann School for the Deaf, where she learned to speak. Her first spoken sentence was: "It is warm."

Her achievement follows Perkins' earlier success with Laura Bridgman, the first deaf and blind person to be given the "key of language."

Alabama-born Keller says she will always be grateful for the support she received in Boston—the "City of Kind Hearts."

YANKEE DIVISION SOLDIERS RETURN HOME AS HEROES

By our defense correspondent
April 26, 1919

SOLDIERS of the U.S. Army's 26th Division came home to a heroes' welcome yesterday after distinguishing themselves in combat during the World War.

Nicknamed the "Yankee Division," it was one of the first American units to arrive in Europe to fight the Germans after U.S. entry into the war. Organized largely from National Guard troops in Massachusetts and other New England states, the division was sent to France as part of the American Expeditionary Forces.

The same division also fought in one of the last major military offensives that helped bring about the Allied defeat of Germany. In total, the 26th Division spent more than 200 days in combat and lost more than 1,500 soldiers who were killed in action.

Privates George Dilboy (circled) and Michael J. Perkins—both of whom lost their lives—will be issued the Medal of Honor for their courageous actions "above and beyond the call of duty."

Dilboy, a Greek-American, was singled out by U.S. forces commander General John Pershing for his "super-human heroism." In total, eight soldiers, sailors, and marines connected to Massachusetts received the Medal of Honor, the highest U.S. military decoration.

Sergeant Stubby, a dog that was a regimental mascot, went to

war with the 26th Division and returned a celebrity. Believed to be part Boston Terrier, he is said to be the war's most decorated dog, having saved American soldiers from surprise gas attacks and once catching a German soldier.

Following the bravery of its armed forces, the U.S. has emerged from the war as a world power. But questions remain as to whether such an enormous cost to human life is really worth the sacrifice.

A GREAT DAY FOR DEMOCRACY

WOMEN WIN RIGHT TO VOTE AFTER LONG STRUGGLE

By our politics editor
June 26, 1919

MASSACHUSETTS yesterday became the eighth U.S. state to approve the 19th Amendment to the U.S. Constitution, giving women the right to vote. The amendment makes it illegal to stop people from voting in national or state elections because of their gender.

The historic event follows years of campaigning by suffragists including Susan B. Anthony—born in the town of Adams—who brought her exceptional skills and energy to the suffragist movement and became president of the National American Woman Suffrage Association.

In 1878, she proposed a revision to an amendment of the U.S. Constitution, giving women the right to vote.

Sadly, Anthony (right), who died in 1906, has not lived to see this day. But the 19th Amendment has come to be known as the "Susan B. Anthony Amendment" in her honor. Other prominent Massachusetts campaigners such as Lucy Stone also passed away before their dream was realized.

Yesterday was nevertheless a great day for democracy—and a great day for women. It follows their important role on the home front during the World War. With so many men away at war, many women worked outside of the home for the first time, filling positions in factories that supported the war effort.

Such patriotic wartime service helped win public support for the suffragist cause. Anna Howard Shaw was the perfect example of

changing times as a female doctor and campaigner who chaired the Women's Committee of the Council of National Defense.

The amendment's passage has not been easy, and President Woodrow Wilson felt compelled to intervene with a U.S. Senate speech. "Give justice to women," he said. The amendment is still to be ratified by other states.

For generations, many men—and even some women—have believed that if women were allowed to take part in politics, they risked neglecting their homes and children.

Suffragists pointed out that women are citizens and should be allowed a voice in government affairs. Despite this, some white campaigners were reluctant to recruit any African-American suffragists due to fears they might deter supporters.

INDIGENOUS women traditionally held various leadership positions in their Native cultures. Successive colonial governments undermined Native women, often rendering them invisible and worthless in other people's minds, as ways of eradicating traditional cultures and obtaining land.

Police strike, seeking better work conditions

MASSACHUSETTS governor Calvin Coolidge has expressed his disgust at the actions of Boston police officers who have been on strike for better wages, *writes our labor relations reporter, September 15, 1919.*

"There is no right to strike against the public safety by anybody, anywhere, anytime," he said.

The strike began in Boston about a week ago when three quarters of the city's police refused to go to work. They were seeking better wages and working conditions as well as union recognition.

But Police Commissioner Edwin Upton Curtis suspended them, and Coolidge called in the Massachusetts National Guard after two nights of rowdy behavior and looting. The Governor's actions have gained him a national reputation.

Amid a public outcry, the officers have ended the strike but new officers will now be recruited to replace them—on higher wages.

The decade is ending as it began: with a rash of strikes. Newspapers have not been sympathetic to the police strike, adopting a very different attitude to their coverage of the "Bread and Roses" Strike of 1912.

Textile workers in Lawrence went on strike against pay cuts for women, linked to enforced shorter hours. The plight of strikers' children sent away from Massachusetts to stay with families attracted national attention.

First Lady Helen Taft took a keen interest, as government investigations revealed the shocking working conditions of immigrant labor.

The dispute united workers of different nationalities through nine cold winter weeks. It ended when mill owners agreed to raise workers' pay.

TRIBAL NATIONS STAND PROUD

By our arts editor
August 12, 1935

THE TRIBAL nations of southern New England are experiencing renewed awareness and pride in their old traditional ways, despite ongoing colonial pressures.

The state terminated the Indian District status of Gay Head and Mashpee, incorporating them into towns in 1870, against the will of the people. Herring Pond tribe became part of the town of Plymouth; and the Nipmuc were declared no longer a tribe in 1869. Laws, however, cannot change who people are—and so they continue.

Traditional governance with chiefs, medicine people, and councils has been reaffirmed.

Mashpee and Herring Pond established an annual powwow in 1921, holding it at Herring Pond the first few years before moving it to Mashpee. Now in its 14th year, the powwow is attended by many tribes from throughout New England. Nipmuc people established their powwow at Hassanamisco in 1924, on land never ceded to the U.S. Along with dancing, singing, drumming, and traditional foods, powwows maintain strong community and kinship ties.

The Gay Headers developed *The Legends of Maushop*, a play based on oral histories handed down generations about a giant who created the Cape and Islands. Community members reenact these ancient stories in Maushop's old home on top of Gay Head's beautiful colored clay cliffs.

CALVIN COOLIDGE—former Governor of Massachusetts and U.S. Vice President—became the 30th President in 1923 after President Warren G. Harding died suddenly. Coolidge presided over the boom years of the "Roaring Twenties" and much of the Prohibition era. A man of few words, "Silent Cal" signed the act granting citizenship to all U.S.-born Native Americans in 1924. His presidency ended on the eve of the Great Depression, which hit people in Massachusetts hard, shutting factories and causing widespread unemployment.

THE BRAINS BEHIND THE BOMB

By our chief reporter
August 16, 1945

SCIENTISTS from the Massachusetts Institute of Technology (MIT) and Harvard in Cambridge have been revealed as members of the secret "Manhattan Project" that built the first atom bombs during World War II.

Everett-born Vannevar Bush (top left), who joined MIT after World War I, initiated the U.S. government project to develop nuclear weapons.

It has also emerged that Harvard played an important role in the development of the bomb.

Harvard University president James Bryant Conant (top middle) became an adviser to the Manhattan Project and to U.S. President Harry Truman, who authorized its use. And J. Robert Oppenheimer— "father of the atomic bomb"—was a Harvard graduate, while Army officer Leslie R. Groves, who oversaw the production and security of the bomb, attended MIT.

The U.S. entered WWII in 1941 when Japan bombed the Pearl Harbor naval base in Hawaii. Nazi Germany was eventually overrun by American and Allied forces. Japan surrendered yesterday, after atom bombs were dropped on two cities, Hiroshima and Nagasaki.

The Japanese surrender has avoided the need for Allied troops to mount what military chiefs predicted would otherwise be a treacherous invasion of the country.

Supported by Britain and Canada, the U.S. recruited some of the world's finest minds to work on the Manhattan Project, whose

WHILE not very well known, the Indigenous people of Massachusetts have taken part in every war that America has been involved in. During the colonial, Revolutionary, and Civil wars, people fought for a variety of reasons. Native people also fought in World Wars I and II, Korean War, Vietnam, Desert Storm, Afghanistan, and Iraq. Pictured above is George Belain, the great-grandson of a whaler. This Aquinnah Wampanoag soldier died in combat at the age of 25 in World War I in France.

secret facility has been revealed at Los Alamos, New Mexico.

In the U.S. armed forces, people from Massachusetts have again achieved an outstanding military record. National Guard troops, who make up a large part of the 26th "Yankee" Infantry Division, fought in France before advancing into Germany and liberating a concentration camp.

About 20 men connected to Massachusetts received Medals of Honor, one of the highest number of decorations for a U.S. state. More than half never returned home.

Among them was Holyoke-born Raymond O. Beaudoin, an Army officer who sacrificed his life to save his men in Germany. Quincy-born U.S. Marine William R. Caddy smothered a grenade blast to protect colleagues at the Battle of Iwo Jima. Wounded Frederick C. Murphy, a Boston-born Army medic, braved a German minefield to treat U.S. soldiers. Killed in an explosion, he saved many lives at the cost of his own.

On the "home front," women often filled the skilled jobs of men who had gone off to fight. More than 8,000 women worked at the Charlestown Navy Yard during the war; 1,000 women worked in Lowell making parachutes.

A cat hat-trick for Dr. Seuss!

A CLEVER new children's book is being hailed a classic by young readers and critics, *writes our culture editor, April 1, 1957.*

The Cat in the Hat is the creation of Theodor Geisel, a children's author and illustrator from Springfield, Massachusetts who writes under the pen name Dr. Seuss. The 236-word story, which took Geisel a year and a half to write, tells the tale of a mischievous cat in a striped hat and bow tie whose attempts to entertain two children left at home on a rainy day accidentally lead to chaos.

The first edition, published on March 1, is proving a phenomenal success thanks to "playground word-of-mouth." Bullock's department store in Los Angeles sold its first 100 copies in a single day. "Hooray for Dr. Seuss!" hollered a headline in the *Chicago Tribune*, after stores in the city could barely keep up with demand.

The Cat in the Hat's anarchic spirit is partly a reaction against the conventional "Dick and Jane" primers traditionally used to teach schoolchildren to read. *LIFE* magazine's John Hersey described Dr. Seuss's infectious and engaging story as a "gift to the art of reading."

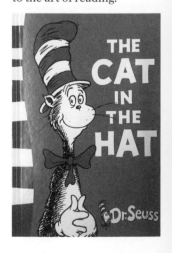

JFK DEATH SHOCKS THE WORLD
BUT THE LEGACY OF SON OF MASSACHUSETTS SET TO LIVE FOREVER

By our chief reporter
November 22, 1963

JOHN F. KENNEDY, 35th U.S. President, was fatally shot earlier today by a hidden gunman as his open-top limousine left downtown Dallas, Texas. The President was rushed to hospital, where frantic efforts were made to save his life, but sadly, he did not survive. He was 46. Mercifully, First Lady Jacqueline Kennedy, who was seated next to her husband, was not hit.

The nation is reeling with horror at the news. Everyone on the streets seems to wear a look of shock and disbelief.

The legacy of this popular Massachusetts politician will surely inspire generations. Kennedy was not only one of the youngest presidents ever but also the first Catholic to hold the office in U.S. history.

Brookline-born "JFK" served as a naval officer in World War II, and was made a hero after saving members of his crew. He went on to represent Massachusetts as a U.S. Congressman and then a U.S. Senator before the presidency.

At his inaugural address,

President Kennedy urged: "... ask not what your country can do for you—ask what you can do for your country."

In May, 1961, he announced to the nation the goal of landing a man on the Moon and returning him safely to Earth before the end of the decade.

In the Cold War era, the world teetered on the brink of nuclear war when the Soviets began constructing missile sites in Cuba. Kennedy said the missiles—capable of reaching U.S. cities must be removed. After a tense standoff with the Soviets, Kennedy got his way.

On a visit to Europe, Kennedy spoke for the free world when he declared "Ich bin ein Berliner" ("I am a Berliner") after visiting the Berlin Wall which the Communists had erected to divide the German city.

One of his most popular achievements has been the Peace Corps, which has sent Americans to underdeveloped countries to fight poverty and disease.

JFK was the son of influential businessman Joseph P. Kennedy, who, as World War II loomed for America, resigned as ambassador to the U.K. over his desire for the U.S. to stay out of the conflict, despite the Nazi threat. "Joe" later devoted his energies to forging a political dynasty led by JFK.

The office of president now falls to Vice President Lyndon B. Johnson. The police, meanwhile, have launched a huge manhunt to find the assassin.

PRESIDENT John F. Kennedy appointed his "inexperienced" brother Robert F. Kennedy to be U.S. Attorney General. "RFK" silenced critics by enforcing civil rights laws, challenging segregation, and combating organized crime. In 1968, less than five years after his brother's death, RFK was tragically assassinated. He was 42.

BOBBI GIBB RUNS INTO THE RECORD BOOKS

BOBBI GIBB became the first woman to complete the Boston Marathon yesterday in an inspiring triumph over prejudice in sport, *writes our sports correspondent, April 20, 1966*.

The 23-year-old Bostonian completed the 26-mile race in three hours, 21 minutes and 40 seconds, finishing ahead of two thirds of the male competitors. Gibb had demonstrated remarkable resolve just to make it to the starting line. After applying for an official place, she received a letter from race director Will Cloney informing her that women were "not physiologically able to run a marathon" and that the race organizers could not "take the liability" of allowing her to compete.

Under the Amateur Athletics Union's rules, women's races are limited to a maximum distance of 1.5 miles (2.4 kilometers). The furthest women are allowed to run in the Olympics is 800 meters.

Gibb, however, was determined to compete. Disguised in a hooded sweatshirt and her brother's Bermuda shorts worn over a black swimsuit, Gibb initially hid in a forsythia bush near the start line. After half the runners had passed, she jumped out and joined the race.

Encouraged by the positive reaction of her fellow runners, Gibb further revealed her identity by taking off the sweatshirt. Spectators shouted their support—"Way to go, girlie!"—and by the time Gibb reached the finish, Massachusetts governor John Volpe was there to shake her hand.

Gibb's achievement prompted a spokesman for the New England Amateur Athletic Union to say he will contact their headquarters to ask for a suspension of the current rules so that any woman can run in the Boston Marathon.

FRANK JAMES SPEAKS OUT

WAMPANOAG LEADER DECLARES "A NATIONAL DAY OF MOURNING"

FRANK "WAMSUTTA" JAMES, an Aquinnah Wampanoag, spoke out yesterday to mark the 350th anniversary of the landing of the Pilgrims, *writes our chief reporter, November 27, 1970.*

James addressed a group of supporters gathered on Cole's Hill near Plymouth Rock, close to a replica of the *Mayflower* and a statue of the 17th-century Wampanoag leader Massasoit.

James had first been asked to write his speech by the Commonwealth of Massachusetts for a 350th anniversary celebration of the supposedly friendly relationship between the early English settlers and the Wampanoag.

When the event organizers read James's speech they thought its critical testimony of the mistreatment of the Wampanoag was inappropriate. James was asked to deliver a revised version, but he refused.

Our reporter was on Cole's Hill to hear James deliver his original speech on the anniversary of what his supporters are now calling a "National Day of Mourning."

"I speak to you as a man—a Wampanoag Man. I am a proud man, proud of my ancestry, my accomplishments.

"It is with mixed emotion that I stand here. This is a time of celebration for you—celebrating an anniversary of a beginning for the white man in America. It is with a heavy heart that I look back upon what happened to my people.

"Even before the Pilgrims landed, it was common practice for explorers to capture Indians, take them to Europe, and sell them as slaves for 220 shillings apiece. The Pilgrims had hardly explored the shores of Cape Cod for four days before they had robbed the graves of my ancestors and stolen their corn and beans.

"Massasoit, the great sachem [leader] of the Wampanoag, knew these facts, yet he and his people welcomed and befriended the settlers of the Plymouth Plantation.

"This action by Massasoit was perhaps our biggest mistake. We, the Wampanoag, welcomed you, the white man, with open arms, little knowing that it was the beginning of the end; that before 50 years were to pass, the Wampanoag would no longer be a free people.

"And so down through the years there is record after record of Indian lands taken and, in token, reservations set up for him upon which to live. The Indian, having been stripped of his power, could only stand by and watch while the white man took his land and used it for his personal gain.

"History wants us to believe that the Indian was a savage, illiterate, uncivilized animal. Let us remember, the Indian is and was just as human as the white man. The Indian feels pain, gets hurt, and becomes defensive, has dreams, bears tragedy and failure ... He, too, is often misunderstood."

IN 1976, two years after the Massachusetts Commission on Indian Affairs was created, Governor Dukakis signed a proclamation giving state recognition to three Massachusetts tribes—the Wampanoag at Gay Head, the Mashpee Wampanoag, and the Nipmuc tribe based in Grafton, MA. The Commission on Indian Affairs continues to represent these tribes and act as a liaison between the state and Indian Peoples.

SCHOOLS BECOME BATTLEGROUND FOR EQUAL RIGHTS

BOSTON schools are in crisis. At South Boston High, there are metal detectors at the doors and state troopers inside, *writes our civil rights correspondent, April 14, 1976.*

The crisis began two years ago when a plan for busing students was introduced to enforce integration in Massachusetts public schools. Earlier, the state legislature ordered them to end segregation, by which African-American and white students attended separate schools.

In a court ruling, U.S. Judge W. Arthur Garrity Jr., found a pattern of racial discrimination in Boston schools. Garrity's ruling means that many African-American and white students will have to attend the same schools for the first time.

Civil rights in America have continued to progress since World War II. Racial segregation has ended within the U.S. armed forces, and laws enacted in the 1960s have made equal rights the law of the land for all Americans.

Schools have become the latest battleground in the struggle for equality. Desegregation has provoked violent racial protests.

Teacher dies in *Challenger* catastrophe

By our space correspondent
January 29, 1986

A MASSACHUSETTS-born teacher was killed yesterday in one of the most tragic days in the history of American space exploration.

The *Challenger* disintegrated off the coast of Cape Canaveral in Florida at 11.39 a.m. EST, just 73 seconds after takeoff. Investigators are already working to establish whether a mechanical fault was to blame for the disaster, possibly connected to the particularly cold weather that accompanied the launch.

The high level of public interest was due to the presence on board of high school teacher Christa McAuliffe, who would have become the first teacher in space.

McAuliffe, who was born in the city of Boston and grew up in Framingham, Massachusetts, was selected by NASA from more than 11,000 applicants to participate in the Teacher in Space Project.

GEORGE H. W. BUSH was elected 41st U.S. President in 1988. The World War II Navy pilot was born in Milton, a Boston suburb, and later moved to Texas, where he made his fortune in the oil industry. Bush was the fifth "son of Massachusetts" to become President, joining John Adams, John Quincy Adams, Calvin Coolidge, and John F. Kennedy.

EXPERT TO REVIVE NATIVE LANGUAGE

A NEW PROJECT to reclaim the Wampanoag language begins today. The language has not been spoken fluently for several generations, *writes our community editor, July 16, 1993.*

Project founder Jessie Little Doe Baird says she began researching the language after having a vision.

Originally an oral language, Wôpanâak is the first Native language to use an alphabetic system and written documents.

Wôpanâak is one of 40 languages of the Algonquian family, and one of only two Native languages left in the state, the other being the Nipmuc language. Prior to European contact and colonization, there were also the Pocumtuk and Mahican languages.

THE WÔPANÂAK Language Reclamation Project (WLRP) operates an immersion school called Mukayuhsak Weekuw for tribal children pre-K through second grade. It also offers elders and elementary after-school classes; three levels of Wôpanâak in the Mashpee High School for any student and continuing community classes.

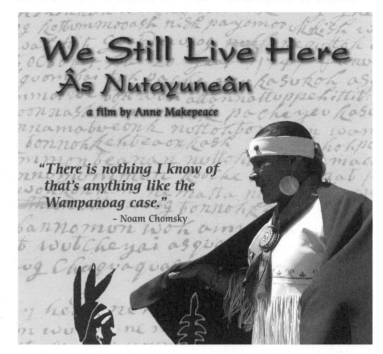

WITHIN MASSACHUSETTS' borders are the ancestral homelands of four Indigenous nations: Wampanoag, Nipmuc, Pocumtuk, Mahican. However, colonial encroachment seized land and disrupted Indigenous ways of life. The largest groups remaining are the Aquinnah Wampanoag (Martha's Vineyard), Mashpee Wampanoag (Cape Cod), Herring Pond Wampanoag (south Plymouth); and the Nipmuc nation (central Mass.). These historic tribes live where they always have, trace direct kinship from pre-contact ancestors, and maintain traditional governments.

Mashpee and Aquinnah are now federally recognized tribes, having direct relationships with the Federal government. Herring Pond and Nipmuc are state recognized. These statutes afford tribes some ability to maintain intact communities after the destruction of colonial processes.

FIRST WOMAN TO BE MADE GOVERNOR!

IN A WATERSHED moment Jane Swift became the first female Governor of Massachusetts yesterday, *writes our political editor, April 11, 2001.*

She succeeds former governor Paul Cellucci after he was appointed ambassador to Canada by President George W. Bush. At 36, Swift is the youngest governor in the United States.

In a special ceremony at the Massachusetts State House, Cellucci handed over several symbols of the state's highest office: a pewter key, a set of statutes from

1860 and a gavel from the celebrated warship USS *Constitution.*

"Transmitted to her excellency Jane Maria Swift on the 10th day of April 2001," Cellucci said. "Thank you for being at my side and good luck leading our great commonwealth." When Cellucci reached the word "her" he was interrupted by cheers and applause. Swift's only words during the ceremony were: "Thank you."

In June, Swift, who grew up in North Adams, expects to become the first state governor in history to give birth while in office, expecting twins.

BOSTON STRONG SPIRIT

CHOCOLATE CHIP COOKIE TURNS 80

THE CITIZENS of Whitman, Massachusetts, will celebrate a momentous event in our state's great history next month: the 80th birthday of the chocolate chip cookie, *writes our food editor, September 28, 2018.*

The inspired combination of cookie dough and chunks of chocolate was invented in 1938 by Ruth Graves Wakefield, the chef and proprietor of the Toll House Inn in Whitman. Originally created as an accompaniment to ice cream, Wakefield's recipe for "Toll House Chocolate Crunch Cookies" first appeared in her *Tried and True* cookbook.

Some accounts of the cookie's creation say it was invented accidentally, as vibrations from a mixer caused chocolate to topple into a batch of dough. Not so, says Wakefield. "We had been serving a thin butterscotch nut cookie with ice cream," she recalls. "Everybody seemed to love it but I was trying to give them something different."

Wakefield's cookie proved such a hit it soon featured on the radio on the popular Betty Crocker cookery show. In 1939, Wakefield gave Nestlé the right to use her recipe and the Toll House name. The price was $1, although Wakefield was reportedly given free chocolate for life.

The cookie's reputation spread during World War II, as troops from Massachusetts stationed overseas received care packages from home and shared their cookies with soldiers from other parts of the United States. Wakefield was soon receiving letters from around the world asking for her recipe: the chocolate chip cookie had gone global.

"NOTHING CAN DEFEAT THE HEART OF THIS CITY"

THE PEOPLE of Boston have shown great courage, resilience, and community spirit this week as the police hunted the suspected perpetrators of the Boston Marathon bombing.

Just five days ago, at 2:50 p.m., two bombs exploded on Boylston Street as crowds of spectators cheered runners approaching the finish line of the popular marathon route.

The blasts killed three people and injured at least 264. The three victims have been named as Martin Richard, an eight-year-old from Dorchester; Krystle Campbell, a 29-year-old from Arlington; and Lingzi Lu, a 23-year-old student.

The city has been in a state of high alert since the manhunt for the bombers began five days ago. The main suspects, Tamerlan and Dzhokhar Tsarnaev, have since claimed a fourth victim: MIT police office Sean Collier, 27, who was shot dead as the brothers tried

By our special reports team
April 20, 2013

to steal his gun.

Last night, Dzhokhar, 19, was discovered by a Watertown resident and taken into custody. Tamerlan, 26, was fatally shot during a gunfight with police. The brothers, both from Cambridge, Massachusetts, are legal immigrants to the United States and of Chechen descent. According to the FBI, the suspects are "not connected to any known terrorist groups."

Despite the fear and violence of recent days, the reaction to the Marathon bombing has shown Boston at its best. From the bravery of the emergency services who rushed to the aid of the victims, to the many acts of kindness shown to strangers by ordinary Bostonians, the city has emerged from the crisis stronger and more united.

This resilience has been

captured in the popular slogan "Boston Strong." Its spirit was invoked in a moving speech delivered yesterday by Mayor Tom Menino.

"Nothing can defeat the heart of this city," said the Mayor. "Nothing will take us down, because we take care of one another."

THE TRAGEDY of the Boston Marathon bombing inspired many extraordinary acts of charity and kindness from the people of Massachusetts. These include the creation of Martin's Park near Boston Children's Museum, opened in 2019 in honor of eight-year-old victim Martin Richard. During "One Boston Day," held on April 15 each year, individuals and groups across the state perform "random acts of kindness and goodwill" to celebrate the spirit of community shown by ordinary people after the bombing.

CENTURY OF SPORTS LEGENDS

By our sports editor
February 4, 2019

THE New England Patriots football team beat the Los Angeles Rams to win the Super Bowl yesterday, matching the record for the most titles. Patriots quarterback Tom Brady, who was featured in all the franchise's triumphs, became the only player in history to win six Super Bowls!

The team's triumph crowns a century or more of sporting excellence in Massachusetts. The Boston Americans baseball team—later renamed the Boston Red Sox—defeated the Pittsburgh Pirates in the first World Series in 1903.

In 2004, the Red Sox ended the "Curse of the Bambino" with a sixth World Series win after an 86-year wait. Fans claimed the "curse" was the result of the sale of star player Babe Ruth. Since then, the team has won three more championships. Ted Williams, who played between 1939 and 1960, is still considered one of the game's greatest hitters.

The Boston Braves—which eventually moved to Atlanta—also won the World Series.

The legendary Boston Celtics basketball team has won 17 championships, more than any other NBA team. One of the Celtics' many great players was Bill Russell, who won 11 NBA championships with the team, and an Olympic medal.

The Boston Bruins, one of North America's "Original Six" ice hockey teams, has won six Stanley Cup championships. The Bruins' Bobby Orr became a legend after scoring a winning shot with a "flying goal." Massachusetts has excelled beyond team sports. Brockton-born Rocky Marciano was the undefeated world heavyweight boxing champion during the 1950s.

The spirit of Massachusetts also burns bright in Olympic sport: Needham-born gymnast Aly Raisman won two gold medals at the Games in 2012 and one in 2016.

The Boston Marathon, said to be the world's oldest annual marathon, was center stage in a "battle of the sexes" in 1966. Bobbi Gibb defied the authorities to become the first woman to run the entire race.

The marathon was a men's division event, and women were not allowed to run in it. Gibb hid in a bush near the start, then quietly joined the race. Later, in a victory for women's equality in sport, the rules were changed to allow women to compete.

STATE TO MARK UNIQUE HERITAGE WITH 400 YEARS' HISTORY

TODAY, Plymouth 400 commemorates a unique heritage that captures the "spirit of America," *writes our culture editor, April 24, 2020.*

The event marks the 400th anniversary of the *Mayflower* voyage and the founding of Plymouth Colony. Earlier this month, the annual Patriots' Day commemorated the Battles of Lexington and Concord, early conflicts of the Revolutionary War that led to American independence.

The story of Massachusetts is the story of America. Its history includes not only Native Americans, Pilgrims and Presidents but also

PLYMOUTH 400™
1620-2020

pioneers of industry, leaders of anti-slavery and women's rights movements. The Wampanoag people are among Native survivors of European colonization, and two of their communities are today federally recognized. Their common

history with English settlers is being fully retold by Plymouth 400's Wampanoag Advisory Committee.

With a diverse population of nearly seven million people, modern Massachusetts is a leader in higher education, technology, and health care. The "Big Dig" under Boston remains one of America's most ambitious highway projects.

"Bay Staters" can draw on a spirit of endurance, innovation, and hard work. In the aftermath of the Boston Marathon bombings, they came together to show solidarity. What will the next 400 years hold?

A TIMELINE GUIDE TO
THE HISTORY OF MASSACHUSETTS

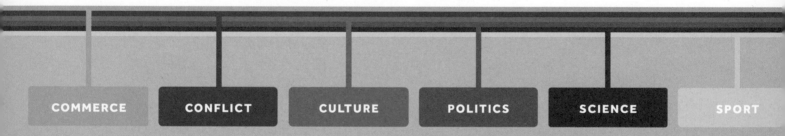

| COMMERCE | CONFLICT | CULTURE | POLITICS | SCIENCE | SPORT |

HOW TO USE THE TIMELINE

Leaf through the pages and travel on an amazing journey to discover key events in the history of Massachusetts, from earliest times to the present day. Each color represents a theme in the story. A selection of important moments in U.S. history helps show the bigger picture and highlights the influence that Massachusetts has had on the nation and beyond.

A series of QR codes run across the middle of the timeline, each one representing a different century over 400 years of history. Focus the camera of a smartphone or tablet on any one of these codes, click on the gray pop-up box and you will be transported to a playlist of videos, made by students, that tell these timeline stories in their own words.

It all adds up to a remarkable story of people and events whose unique legacy can still be felt today in the sixth State of the Union.

PLYMOUTH 400™
1620-2020

MASSACHUSETTS
FROM EARLIEST TIMES TO THE PRESENT DAY

About 12,000 years ago
MASSACHUSETTS is an ancient land. People move into North America's northeast after an ice age, which shapes its distinctive coastline. They hunt caribou and small animals. Adapting to their environments, humans hunt in the forests and fish the abundant waterways. Later, people will live in villages and start growing crops.

About 5,000 years ago
NATIVE people live in Quonehassit harbor, site of modern-day Boston, building huge **weirs** to trap fish. Massachusett, Nipmuc, and Wampanoag people are among Native groups, whose complex societies often include female elders. "Massachusetts" is a Native word thought to mean "near the great hills," from which the state gets its name.

1620
SICK and weary after weeks at sea, the *Mayflower* Pilgrims land in New England, north of their intended destination. Off modern-day Provincetown, they sign a compact, agreeing to a self-governing body to create "just and equal" laws. The Mayflower **Compact** is an early example of democracy in America.

1620
A GROUP of English **Separatists**—including some who earlier migrated to Holland—set sail from Plymouth, England, for North America in the *Mayflower*. The "Pilgrims" are making this grueling journey to establish a colony with the freedom to practice religion as they want.

1621
MASSASOIT, whose Wampanoag people are depleted by disease and threatened by rival Native groups, makes an alliance with the Pilgrims. He has reason to be suspicious of them at first: before their arrival, Europeans kidnapped Native Americans and sold them into slavery.

1623
PLYMOUTH COLONY is credited as the first place in America to establish trial by jury. Its legislature, the General Court, rules that all criminal cases, as well as matters of **trespass** and debt, should be tried by 12 "honest men" in the form of a jury. It is a milestone in American legal history.

1630
A LARGE group of **Puritans** leave England for New England. John Winthrop says the Massachusetts Bay Colony will be like a "City upon a Hill" with "the eyes of all people" upon them. The Puritans believe they are heading for a "Promised Land," and Winthrop will be the colony's most influential governor.

1600s

1620s

1630s

~5,000 years ago

1614
JOHN SMITH, an early leader of an English settlement in Virginia, sails from Maine to Cape Cod, exploring the coastline. He names the region "New England," reporting that it is blessed with an "excellent climate" and promotes it as an ideal location for **colonization**. European fishermen had visited the region for decades, but did not settle.

1618
NATIVE villages along the New England coast are virtually wiped out at the height of a plague. A combination of diseases hits local populations. The epidemic started in 1616 and is said to have been spread by European traders and fishermen. Later it will be called the "great dying."

1620
THE PILGRIMS establish Plymouth Colony on the site where a Patuxet village ravaged by disease once stood. The harbor is shallow and there is a plentiful supply of clean spring water. In the midst of winter, they rapidly build homes for shelter. Samoset, a Native man who speaks some English, will visit the settlement and bid them welcome.

1630
THE PURITANS arrive in Massachusetts Bay and search for a place to settle. They select the Shawmut Peninsula. The name "Boston" is said to have been chosen by Isaac Johnson, a colonist who once lived in the English town of Boston.

1621
THE FIRST winter in Plymouth Colony claims the lives of many Pilgrims. Tisquantum, or "Squanto," a Native man, shows survivors where to fish and how to plant corn using fish as a fertilizer. He spent several years in England after being kidnapped, and becomes the translator between the Pilgrims and the Wampanoag people.

1621
DESPITE many hardships, Plymouth Colony survives, led by Governor William Bradford. About 50 Pilgrims celebrate with a feast and about 90 Native people join them. The Pilgrims hunt **"fowl"**—including turkeys; Native people bring deer. The event inspires today's annual national Thanksgiving.

1635
BOSTON LATIN SCHOOL is the first public school in America, with a subscription raised for a schoolmaster. Later, Native people will be taught free of charge. Early students are John Hancock, Samuel Adams, Benjamin Franklin, William Hooper, and Robert Treat Paine, all signers of the U.S. **Declaration of Independence**.

A series of QR codes along the middle of the timeline represents each century. Point your smartphone or tablet camera on any QR code to see video-shorts made by students. Click on the QR code on the right to visit the *Massachusetts Chronicles* website.

See pages 46–48 for a useful Glossary (caption words marked in red)

1637
PURITAN leaders in Massachusetts become intolerant of other religious groups and banish those whose beliefs are different from their own. Anne Hutchinson defends her right, as a Christian woman, to preach in Boston. She is expelled and will settle in what is today Rhode Island, whose principal founder, Roger Williams, is also expelled.

1636
A COLLEGE is founded by the Massachusetts Bay Colony across the Charles River from Boston. It will be named for John Harvard, a minister who donates his library and much of his fortune. Harvard is located in "Cambridge" after the English university, and will become a world center of learning.

1660
MEMBERS of the **Quaker** religion are hanged after refusing to be banished by Boston's Puritans. Mary Dyer goes to her death for repeatedly re-entering Massachusetts. After the Quaker victims are hailed **martyrs**, Puritans slowly begin to tolerate other religious groups.

1691
THE BORDERS of Massachusetts begin to take shape. The Province of Massachusetts Bay is declared a colony of the English Crown, and will join up with Plymouth Colony. Maine is part of Massachusetts, but will later become a U.S. state. A royal **charter** allows voting based on property rather than religious qualifications.

THE
CHARTER
Granted by Their Majesties
King WILLIAM
AND
Queen MARY,
TO THE
INHABITANTS

1692
DESPITE professing their innocence, 20 men and women are executed for witchcraft in Salem. Those who confess are spared. Their accusers include an enslaved woman and children gripped by fits. **"Spectral evidence"** sends the accused to the gallows, till the witch hunts are stopped.

1722
BENJAMIN FRANKLIN, one of the **Founding Fathers**, spends his early life in Massachusetts. Born in Boston, he attends the Latin School, though he does not graduate. The future statesman and inventor flees to Philadelphia in a controversy over free speech. He will later discover electricity in lightning.

1764
THE BRITISH government taxes its American colonies to help pay for the costly **French and Indian War.** Lawyer James Otis Jr. criticizes taxation without representation, fueling opposition to British rule. Later he will attack the Stamp Act which imposes a tax on printed materials.

1768
AS BOSTON edges toward open revolt against Britain's colonial rule and its tax measures, British troops— known as **redcoats**—parade through the city streets, angering many citizens who say their liberties are being ignored. Many colonists see the soldiers' presence as an act of hostility.

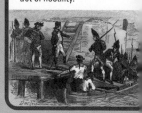

1650s   1660s   1670s   1690s   [QR code] 1700s   1730s   1760s

1651
PURITANS establish "Praying Towns" to convert Native peoples in Massachusetts to Christianity and controversially, replace their ancient way of life. With the help of Native people, John Eliot translates the Bible into the Wampanoag language, the first complete Bible printed in America.

1720
WITH a population of 12,000, Boston is boosted by the slave trade. Merchants load ships with rum and other goods in Boston, which are then sold in Europe. Profits are used to buy enslaved people in Africa, who are transported to plantations in the Caribbean—a tragic chapter in history.

1733
PREACHER Jonathan Edwards helps to lead the Great Awakening from his church in Northampton. As part of the religious movement, **evangelical** preachers actively seek to convert others to Christianity, regardless of race or gender. Edwards reports that young people are waking up to God.

1639
LONDON-BORN Stephen Daye is credited as the first printer in colonial North America after moving to Massachusetts. He prints the *Oath of a Freeman*, a pledge made by members of the **Massachusetts Bay Company**. His *Whole Booke of Psalmes* (the "Bay Psalm Book") is said to be the first book published in the North American colonies.

THE
VVHOLE
BOOKE OF PSALMES
Faithfully
TRANSLATED *into* ENGLISH
Metre.
Whereunto is prefixed a discourse de-

1675
CONFLICT erupts in King Philip's War. Metacom (King Philip), son of Massasoit, fights to protect his Native people and ancestral lands from further colonization. Native and colonial towns are destroyed. Metacom is killed— his head displayed on a **pike** in Plymouth for 25 years. Many Native families are enslaved.

[British flag]
COLONIAL AMERICA
IN BRITAIN'S global empire are 13 English-speaking colonies in North America. With the support of American colonists who serve as militias, Britain defeats France in the French and Indian War (or Seven Years' War), and gains Canadian territories in 1763. Britain angers American colonists by imposing taxes to pay for the war, a major cause of the American Revolution.

1765
MASSACHUSETTS plays a vital role in the American Revolution. Boston-born Samuel Adams is said to be a founder of the Sons of Liberty **patriot** group. Rejecting Britain's authority to tax the American colonies without their consent, he calls on them to unite in opposition.

1773
PHILLIS WHEATLEY, an enslaved woman, is the first African-American female poet to be published in Britain and the U.S. colonies. Purchased as a servant, she was educated by the Wheatley family. She eventually conquers the literary scene and also gains her freedom.

1775
THE BRITISH win the Revolutionary War's first major conflict, but the Battle of Bunker Hill, at Charlestown, is costly. Earlier, colonial forces had dug in on nearby Breed's Hill, but retreat to Bunker Hill after several British assaults. The conflict confirms the need for the **Continental Army**.

AMERICAN REVOLUTION
THE 13 COLONIES eventually unite against Britain, declaring independence in 1776. Lacking representation in British government, the colonists reject Britain's right to tax them. With French and Spanish help, the American colonies defeat the British. The Revolutionary War ends in 1783, and the United States of America is established. A new constitution creates a federal system of national government.

1786
AN UPRISING is led by Revolutionary War veteran Daniel Shays. Struggling to cope with tax and debt levels, farmers will march on a Springfield armory. Shays' Rebellion exposes weaknesses in national government, influencing a convention that creates the U.S. Constitution.

1773
IN A DARING protest against British rule, patriots—some disguised as Native American warriors—dump hundreds of chests full of British tea into Boston Harbor. The "Boston Tea Party" is a direct challenge to Britain and its unpopular "tea tax" on the colonies, which has become a symbol of Britain's right to govern.

1775
AT 10 P.M. on April 18, craftsman-turned-patriot Paul Revere races from Boston to Lexington to warn patriots that the redcoats are coming. British troops detain him before he reaches nearby Concord, but he is eventually let go. With the help of fellow patriots, his famous "midnight ride" spreads the word.

1776
A BRITISH fleet leaves Boston Harbor with thousands of troops aboard. The siege of British-occupied Boston is over, and George Washington's Continental Army has its first victory. His men had taken the hills overlooking the city, and the British had evacuated rather than risk a bloody battle like the one at Bunker Hill.

1776
ABIGAIL ADAMS, wife of John Adams, and their children are inoculated against smallpox. The treatment follows experiments by Boston's Zabdiel Boylston, who inoculates his son and others, though some die. Later, Harvard Medical School cofounder Benjamin Waterhouse will test a safer cowpox vaccine.

1770s

1780s

1775
THE FIRST shots of the Revolutionary War are fired at Lexington and Concord. The conflict at Lexington claims eight colonists' lives. At Concord, patriots battle redcoats at North Bridge and gain the upper hand. As they retreat, the British are ambushed: 73 redcoats and 49 patriots are killed.

1776
DELEGATES to the Continental Congress sign the Declaration of Independence—an act of treason in British eyes. Massachusetts signers include John Adams, Samuel Adams and John Hancock, Congress president. To this day, the expression, "Put your John Hancock on it," is a way of asking for a person's signature.

1781
USING the state constitution, slavery is effectively abolished in Massachusetts after a series of court cases. In two legal challenges, Elizabeth Freeman and Quock Walker win their freedom. In time, the Commonwealth will play a key role in the **abolition movement** to end slavery throughout the U.S.

1770
BRITISH soldiers kill five colonists and injure others in the Boston Massacre. Earlier, a mob dares the soldiers to shoot. Crispus Attucks, a man of color, is among the dead. Support for the American Revolution grows. To uphold law and order, John Adams, second cousin of Samuel Adams, will defend the British soldiers in court.

1775
THE BRITISH declare Massachusetts to be in a state of rebellion. They regard armed colonists as "traitors" and order General Thomas Gage to use force to stop them from stockpiling weapons. Patriots, meanwhile, set up **Minutemen** companies of about 50 men each. Conflict appears unavoidable.

1775
MASSACHUSETTS delegate to the **Continental Congress**, John Adams, nominates George Washington to command the newly created Continental Army. Arriving in Cambridge, Washington calls his troops "an exceedingly nasty and dirty people." His challenge is to turn the men into a formidable force.

1780
MASSACHUSETTS creates a **constitution**, declaring that all men are born "free and equal." Many believe the new "Commonwealth" abolishes slavery, making it illegal. But voting rights do not extend to women. Drafted by John Adams, it is now the world's oldest functioning written constitution.

1797
JOHN ADAMS—a Founding Father, first ambassador to Britain, and first U.S. Vice President—succeeds first U.S. President George Washington, defeating Thomas Jefferson to be elected second U.S. President. The Massachusetts lawyer will eventually move into the newly built White House in Washington, D.C.

1803
MASSACHUSETTS is a pioneer of America's **Industrial Revolution**. The Middlesex Canal connects the Merrimack River to Boston—one of the first engineering projects of its kind—and other canals follow, as well as early railroads. The Chain Bridge at Newburyport will be the first suspension bridge in the U.S.

U.S. EXPANSION
THE U.S. expands in 1803 after buying the Louisiana Territory from France. The War of 1812 settles its northeastern border with British-controlled Canada. Later, the U.S. will acquire Florida from Spain, and take over Texas. It will defeat Mexico in a war and gain vast lands, including California—the climax of the belief in "Manifest Destiny" that U.S. expansion across the continent is certain to happen, and desirable, even at the expense of Native peoples.

1827
EDGAR ALLAN POE's first book of poetry is published without his name on it. The book is credited only to a "Bostonian." Poe was orphaned as a child and served for a time in the U.S. Army at Fort Independence in Boston Harbor. The poet and master storyteller will become world famous.

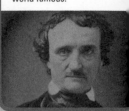

1788
MASSACHUSETTS approves the U.S. Constitution—the body of laws that will govern the newly independent United States—and becomes the 6th U.S. state. Its politicians play a key role in shaping the national constitution, though Elbridge Gerry refuses to sign as it does not then include a **Bill of Rights**.

1798
THE MASSACHUSETTS State House is completed in Boston. Designed by Charles Bulfinch, the elegant **state capitol** building is constructed on land once owned by John Hancock, the Commonwealth's first elected governor. A time capsule by Samuel Adams and Paul Revere is buried in the building.

1816
HENRY HALL, of Dennis, begins commercial cultivation of cranberries after discovering they grow better when sand is spread over them. Others adopt his technique, and "Cranberry Fever" grips Cape Cod as the industry booms. Long before European settlers, Wampanoag people enjoyed wild cranberries.

1790s — **1800s** — **1810s** — **1820s** — **1830s**

1790
THE *COLUMBIA* sailing ship is built in Massachusetts—the first U.S. vessel to travel around the world. It is said to give its name to British Columbia, a Canadian province. Later, the Command-Service Module of *Apollo 11*—which achieved the first manned Moon landing—and a NASA space shuttle will also take the ship's name.

1797
THE *CONSTITUTION*, a 44-gun warship, is launched in Boston. U.S. Congress orders the ship and several others to be part of a new national navy, which will protect American vessels from French **privateers** and pirate raids. In the War of 1812, it will earn the nickname "Old Ironsides" after defeating a British warship.

1812
WAR BREAKS out between the U.S. and Britain over maritime rights, a conflict strongly opposed by Massachusetts. Coastal towns including Boston suffer a British naval blockade and forts are strengthened. The War of 1812 actually lasts until 1815, ending in stalemate.

1831
ABOLITIONIST William Lloyd Garrison publishes *The Liberator*, a Boston newspaper that calls for the emancipation of all slaves in the U.S. Garrison, a white man born in Newburyport, is a founder of the American Anti-Slavery Society, inspiring many African-Americans to make their voices heard.

1814
FACTORIES are springing up across Massachusetts, producing tools and paper, wool, and cotton textiles. Francis Cabot Lowell's mill in Waltham is the first in the U.S. to turn raw cotton into finished cloth, all under one roof. The city of Lowell will be a center of the new age, named for this pioneer of industry.

1795
SPRINGFIELD Armory makes the first musket in the U.S. Springfield was chosen by George Washington as the site of the patriots' armory during the Revolutionary War, and later, was a target of Shays' Rebellion. Springfield muskets and rifles will become world famous.

1825
JOHN QUINCY ADAMS, a diplomat, and son of Founding Father John Adams, becomes the sixth U.S. President. He was chosen by the U.S. House of Representatives after all four candidates failed to win an electoral majority. He is named after John Quincy, a great-grandfather, for whom the city of Quincy is also named.

1844
ABOLITIONIST campaigners are drawn to "forward-thinking" Massachusetts. Sojourner Truth, who was born into slavery, joins a community in Northampton, while John Brown, a white man, moves to Springfield. Boston's Beacon Hill becomes a center for free African-Americans and escaped enslaved people.

1845
THOUSANDS of starving Irish people begin immigration to America after the failure of their country's potato crop. Previously the Irish came to Massachusetts to build canals and railroads or work in factories, but not in such great numbers. Many settle in cities such as Boston, but endure anti-Catholic prejudice and a life of poverty.

1851
COMMERCIAL whaling off Nantucket island dates back to the 17th century. As the industry expands, ports such as New Bedford flourish. The hunt for whales is brilliantly captured in Herman Melville's classic story *Moby Dick; or, The Whale*. Commercial whaling is banned in the U.S. in the 1970s.

1861
AS America's industrial power grows, the Massachusetts Institute of Technology is established to further scientific advances. It will become one of the world's top educational institutions, famed for research and world-class experts such as Tim Berners-Lee, inventor of the World Wide Web.

1861
JULIA WARD HOWE, a Boston resident, writes the "Battle Hymn of the Republic" after meeting President Abraham Lincoln. Earlier, she married the founder of what is now Perkins School for the Blind. Helping to lead the Massachusetts Woman Suffrage Association, she will campaign for a "Mother's Day" for world peace.

AMERICAN CIVIL WAR
ONE of the bloodiest wars in U.S. history starts in 1861 after 11 Southern states break away from the Union. They fear President Abraham Lincoln will ban slavery, on which their farming economy is built. Lincoln issues the Emancipation Proclamation in 1863, declaring that slaves in rebel states are free. The war ends two years later, with the Union restored and slavery ended. But Lincoln is assassinated and the southern states are devastated by war.

1837
MASSACHUSETTS becomes a leader in public education, championed by its new education secretary Horace Mann. As a result, teacher training colleges are established for the first time, such as Bridgewater Normal School (1840), later becoming Bridgewater State University.

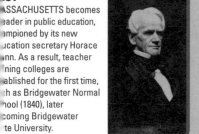

1846
A DEMONSTRATION by Dr. William T. G. Morton uses ether gas to make a patient unconscious during surgery. But the Harvard Medical School dentist, born in Charlton, will anger professional colleagues, who regard as selfish his pursuit of a **patent** that could make him a fortune from his discovery.

1840s

1850s

1860s

1870s

1833
MASHPEE Wampanoag leaders protest at the state's running of their reservation, and are angry at the theft of wood from their forests. The Mashpee Revolt, led by Native American preacher William Apess, will win back some self-rule, but Native property rights are seldom enforced.

1854
HENRY DAVID THOREAU spends two years living beside Walden Pond, near Concord. The land is owned by fellow **transcendentalist** Ralph Waldo Emerson. Thoreau describes his simple living in a book titled *Walden; or, Life in the Woods*, and is an inspiration to the early environmental movement.

1868
LOUISA MAY ALCOTT, daughter of transcendentalist Amos Bronson Alcott, pens the famous novel *Little Women*, the story of teenage sisters growing up in rural Massachusetts. She gains instruction from celebrated family friends, such as Ralph Waldo Emerson and Henry David Thoreau.

1845
JOHN CHAPMAN, better known as folk hero "Johnny Appleseed," dies. Born and raised in Leominster, he left Massachusetts for the Midwest, where settlers were starting farms. He became a legend after planting apple tree nurseries. In keeping with his nickname, he is said to have carried apple seeds on his travels.

1850
THE FIRST annual National Women's Rights Convention is held in Worcester. Lucy Stone, of West Brookfield—the first woman from Massachusetts to earn a college degree—is one of the main organizers. At the historic gathering, delegates hear speeches on women's suffrage, equal wages, and property rights.

1863
THE 54th and 55th Massachusetts Volunteers are among the first regiments of armed African-Americans to be organized by the northern states to fight in the Civil War. Men of the 54th are praised for their bravery when, with other **Union** regiments, they storm Fort Wagner in South Carolina. Many are killed or wounded.

1870
THE MASHPEE and Aquinnah Wampanoag communities become citizens of Massachusetts when their reservations are incorporated as towns. They are given the right to own and sell their land without the need for state-appointed guardians. This further threatens the loss of the tribes' common lands.

1845
FREDERICK DOUGLASS gains a national reputation after his first autobiography is published, describing his earlier life as an enslaved man. Living for a time in New Bedford and Lynn, he is inspired by *The Liberator* newspaper of William Lloyd Garrison, and will become a national abolitionist leader.

1872
A SPARK from a steam-powered boiler ignites the Great Fire of Boston. Hundreds of buildings are destroyed, including many commercial warehouses. The fire ruins the city's wool trade and wrecks shoe and paper businesses. At least 20,000 girls are put out of work. The city creates new building regulations.

1878
SUFFRAGIST Susan B. Anthony, born in Adams, proposes a revision to an amendment of the U.S. Constitution, giving women the right to vote. Known as the "Susan B. Anthony Amendment," it will not become law until 1920—as the 19th Amendment. She will be the first woman to appear on a U.S. coin.

1890
THE POEMS of Emily Dickinson, a resident of Amherst, are published after her death, revealing her talents as a major U.S. author. She wrote almost entirely in private, preferring to avoid society. Now her secret is out, confirming once again that Massachusetts is a literary powerhouse.

1909
AS "JIM CROW" laws enforce racial **segregation** in the South, civil rights leader W.E.B. Du Bois cofounds the National Association for the Advancement of Colored People, which works for equal rights for people of all races. Born in Great Barrington, he is the first African American to earn a Harvard doctorate degree.

PROHIBITION
THE 18th Amendment to the U[nited States] Constitution—and the 1920 Vols[tead] Act, which makes the amendm[ent] an enforceable law—bans the [sale] of alcoholic beverages in an att[empt] to curb crime and poverty. Fed[eral] agents try to enforce the law[,] but organized crime gangs ma[ke] fortunes from illegal alcohol sa[les.] Prohibition is ended in 1933.

1881
THE BOSTON Symphony Orchestra (BSO) gives its first concert. Later, it will become one of America's "Big Five" symphony orchestras. Lawrence-born Leonard Bernstein, who writes the music for the famous musical *West Side Story*, will be among many world-class conductors to make recordings with the "BSO."

1903
THE BOSTON Americans baseball team—later renamed the "Red Sox"—defeats the Pittsburgh Pirates in the first World Series. The champions of the American and National Leagues meet in a post-season showdown. The Huntington Avenue Grounds in Boston are mobbed by fans after the Americans' victory.

1880s

1890s

1900s

1910s

1876
A NEW era in communications begins when Alexander Graham Bell invents the first practical telephone after transmitting the human voice by wire. The Boston University professor, who works with deaf people, is awarded a patent for his invention. A call from Salem to Boston is one of the earliest over a long distance.

1886
WORKING with engineer George Westinghouse, physicist William Stanley Jr. demonstrates his Alternating Current (AC) electrical system to light offices and stores in Great Barrington. His AC system allows electrical power to be distributed over wide areas, winning the **"War of the Currents"** with Thomas Edison.

1904
HELEN KELLER is one of the first deaf-blind people to earn a college degree—from Radcliffe women's college, today part of Harvard University. Her autobiography tells the inspiring story of how, with the help of her teacher and companion Anne Sullivan, she learns to read, write, and speak.

1881
CLARA BARTON, born in North Oxford, founds the American Red Cross. A nurse in the Civil War, she collected medical supplies for Union soldiers, and became known as the "Angel of the Battlefield." Under her leadership, the movement responds to humanitarian crises. A U.S. commemorative stamp will honor her.

WORLD WAR I
THE U.S. abandons neutrality in 1917, and declares war on the German Empire after public outrage at American deaths from submarine warfare. The 26th "Yankee" Division is formed largely from the Massachusetts National Guard, and is among the first to be sent to France as part of the American Expeditionary Forces. Germany is defeated, and the U.S. emerges as a world power.

1912
TEXTILE workers in Lawren[ce] strike against pay cuts for women, linked to enforced shorter hours. The plight of strikers' children sent away to stay with families gains widespread attention. The "Bread and Roses" Strike unites immigrant labor, and mill owners end the dispute by raising workers' pay.

1891
TO KEEP students active in winter, gym teacher James Naismith invents basketball in Springfield. Students throw a large ball into peach baskets suspended from a balcony. The game will become one of the world's most popular sports. Later, physical education director William G. Morgan invents volleyball in nearby Holyoke.

1919
GEORGE HERMAN RUTH JR.— Babe "The Bambino" Ruth—is a star player for the Boston Red Sox baseball team. After the Sox sell Ruth to the New York Yankees, he leads the Yankees to four World Series victories. Sox fans blame the "Curse of the Bambino" for their team's failure to win a World Series for 86 years.

1926
WORCESTER-BORN Robert H. Goddard, a Clark University physicist, develops a liquid-fueled rocket that kicks off the Space Age. Goddard launches the rocket high into the sky in Auburn, and will be recognized as a pioneer of rocketry. He inspires an age of space flight and the development of new weapons of war.

1966
EDWARD BROOKE, a graduate of Boston University School of Law, becomes the first African-American elected to the U.S. Senate by popular vote, where he represents Massachusetts. He champions the causes of low-income housing and an increased minimum wage.

1918
AT THE Cape Cod seaside town of Orleans, a German submarine carries out the only attack on U.S. soil during World War I. The submarine fires at the tugboat *Perth Amboy*, sinking several barges it is towing. Aircraft fire back, attempting to bomb the submarine. Enemy shells land in a marsh and on a beach.

1923
CALVIN COOLIDGE—former U.S. Vice President and Governor of Massachusetts— becomes the 30th U.S. President, after President Warren G. Harding dies suddenly. Presiding over the boom years of the "Roaring Twenties," he will sign an act granting citizenship to all U.S.-born Native Americans.

WORLD WAR II
THE U.S. enters World War II in 1941 when Japan bombs the Pearl Harbor naval base in Hawaii. Some 16 million soldiers serve in the American armed forces, and 400,000 are killed in action. In 1945, the U.S. becomes the world's first superpower when Nazi Germany is overrun, and Japan surrenders after atom bombs are dropped on two cities, Hiroshima and Nagasaki.

1957
SPRINGFIELD-BORN Theodor "Dr. Seuss" Geisel publishes *The Cat in the Hat*, one of more than 60 children's books that he writes and illustrates. His stories, such as *How the Grinch Stole Christmas*, are among the most popular children's works of all time. A museum in Springfield will honor him.

1962
EDWARD M. KENNEDY, known as "Ted," serves for decades as a U.S. Senator from Massachusetts. The brother of JFK and RFK, Ted continues the family's political tradition. A personal scandal will harm his chances of becoming President, but he earns a legacy as one of America's most respected Senators.

1920s — **1940s** — **1950s** — **1960s**

1919
A GIANT tank filled with more than two million gallons of molasses explodes, releasing a "tidal wave" of the syrupy substance 50 feet high and swamping a Boston neighborhood. The Great Molasses Flood is a major industrial accident, claiming 21 lives and injuring dozens more.

1942
THE MASSACHUSETTS National Guard, which forms a large part of the U.S. Army's 26th "Yankee" Infantry Division, will fight in Europe during World War II. Twenty-two men connected to Massachusetts will receive the Medal of Honor. The conflict also comes close to home: a Nazi submarine sinks ships off Provincetown, killing 93.

1961
PRESIDENT Kennedy hires his brother Robert F. Kennedy. Appointed U.S. Attorney General, "RFK" challenges organized crime and segregation. In the era of the civil rights movement, he champions laws to halt discrimination. Tragically, in 1968, RFK will also be assassinated like his brother.

WOMEN'S SUFFRAGE
IN 1920, the 19th Amendment to the U.S. Constitution is officially adopted, giving women the right to vote in national elections. It follows their important role on the "Home Front" in World War I, when many women worked in transport or arms factories. Campaigners include the National American Woman Suffrage Association and Alice Paul's militant party, whose members are arrested for picketing the White House. Massachusetts is the 8th U.S. state to approve the amendment.

THE NEW DEAL
U.S. PRESIDENT Franklin D. Roosevelt launches the "New Deal" in 1933, creating jobs and relief for Americans hardest hit by the Great Depression—the worst financial slump in modern times. The program includes employment projects, experimental social welfare, and insurance programs to get America back on its feet. The Depression hits many Massachusetts industries, including textiles and shoemaking.

1960
JOHN F. KENNEDY is elected 35th President, the first Catholic to hold the office and one of the youngest ever Presidents. "JFK" is a World War II hero who represented Massachusetts as a Congressman and then a Senator. The nation reels in horror when he is later **assassinated** while in office, aged 46.

1966
ROBERTA LOUISE "BOBBI" GIBB defies the authorities to become the first woman to run the entire Boston Marathon. The marathon is a men's division race, and women are not allowed to run in it. Gibb hides in a bush near the start, then quietly joins the race. Later, the rules will be changed to allow women to compete.

1970

THE BOSTON BRUINS hockey team defeats the St. Louis Blues to win their fourth Stanley Cup championship. Bobby Orr becomes a legend after scoring the winning shot with a "flying goal." The Bruins are one of the "Original Six" hockey teams and will go on to future Stanley Cup victories.

2001

JANE SWIFT, who grew up in North Adams, serves as acting Governor of Massachusetts and is the first woman to hold the office. She is also the first governor to give birth while in office. She leads education reforms and campaigns to create the Department of Homeland Security after the September 11 terrorist attacks.

What will be the key events of tomorrow? See how today's students imagine their future!

CIVIL RIGHTS MOVEMENT

THE STRUGGLE for equal rights for people of all races is inspired by Rosa Parks in 1955 after she refuses to give up her bus seat for a white person. Martin Luther King Jr., who received a doctoral degree from Boston University, later makes his famous "I Have a Dream" speech in Washington, D.C., imagining a world in which all people are treated equally. He is assassinated in 1968.

1970

FRANK "WAMSUTTA" JAMES of the Aquinnah Wampanoag tribe is asked to speak at the 350th anniversary of the *Mayflower* voyage. His remarks are censored and instead he makes his speech in Plymouth on Thanksgiving Day, sparking a trend for tribes to observe a National Day of Mourning instead of a Thanksgiving holiday.

1988

GEORGE H. W. BUSH is elected 41st U.S. President. The World War II Navy pilot was born in Milton, and later moved to Texas. During his presidency, the Soviet Union collapses, he launches the Gulf War, and he negotiates an important North American trade agreement.

2010

A CENSUS finds 37,000 Native Americans living in Massachusetts. Wampanoag and Nipmuc people are among survivors of European colonization. They continue to maintain their cultural traditions and work to raise awareness of historical injustices.

2019

THE Massachusetts-based New England Patriots football team defeats the Los Angeles Rams, matching the National Football League (NFL) record for the most Super Bowl titles. Patriots quarterback Tom Brady becomes the only player in history to win six Super Bowls! In another historic moment, the first male cheerleaders perform.

1970s — **1980s** — **2000s** — **2010s**

1966

THE BOSTON Celtics basketball team defeats the Los Angeles Lakers to win their eighth NBA title in a row. The Celtics will go on to win a total of 17 championships, more than any other team in the NBA. Over the years, the team's greatest stars have included Bill Russell, John Havlicek, Kevin McHale, Larry Bird, and Paul Pierce.

1986

THE SPACE SHUTTLE *Challenger* explodes after takeoff, killing all seven astronauts aboard, including Boston-born Christa McAuliffe, who was to have been the first schoolteacher in space. In total, a dozen or more astronauts have come from Massachusetts. Others studied at MIT, including Buzz Aldrin.

2013

ON APRIL 15, two homemade bombs claim lives and injure many others at the Boston Marathon. Citizens adopt the slogan "Boston Strong" and an annual "One Boston Day" will be launched for people to donate food, give blood, or perform other acts of kindness for victims, their families, and others in need.

THE COLD WAR

THE U.S. backs nations threatened by Soviet expansion after World War II. Decades of tense nuclear-armed stand-off follow, with Europe divided by the "Iron Curtain." The world narrowly escapes nuclear war when Russia plans to base missiles in Cuba. America will fight costly wars in Korea and—amid popular protests—Vietnam. The Cold War ends with the Soviet Union's collapse in 1991.

1974

AFTER the Massachusetts legislature ordered public schools to end segregation, a federal judge in Boston orders **busing** students to enforce **integration**. Many African-American and white students attend the same schools for the first time, but busing provokes riots in Boston.

WAR ON TERROR

ON SEPTEMBER 11, 2001, hijackers use airliners to launch suicide attacks. Thousands are killed or injured, including more than 150 passengers and crew on two planes that take off from Boston's Logan International Airport. Responding to the slaughter, President George W. Bush declares a "war on terror."

2004

MASSACHUSETTS becomes the first U.S. state to legalize same-sex marriage. It follows a landmark legal decision by its Supreme Judicial Court that to bar same-sex couples from marriage violates the Massachusetts Constitution, which declares the equality of all individuals. Thousands of same-sex couples marry.

2020

WITH a diverse population of nearly seven million "Bay Staters," Massachusetts is a leader in higher education, technology, and health care. A series of anniversaries will commemorate its rich heritage—from Plymouth 400 and Thanksgiving to the founding of Boston and its role in the American Revolution.

ABOUT MASSACHUSETTS

State name: Commonwealth of Massachusetts
Before statehood: Province of Massachusetts Bay
State capital: Boston
State motto: *Ense petit placidam sub libertate quietem* (Latin)—"By the sword we seek peace, but peace only under liberty"
State nicknames: The Bay State, the Pilgrim State, the Puritan State, the Baked Bean State
State song: "All Hail to Massachusetts"
State flower: Mayflower
State bird: Chickadee
State fish: Atlantic cod
State beverage: Cranberry juice
State dog: Boston Terrier
State reptile: Garter snake

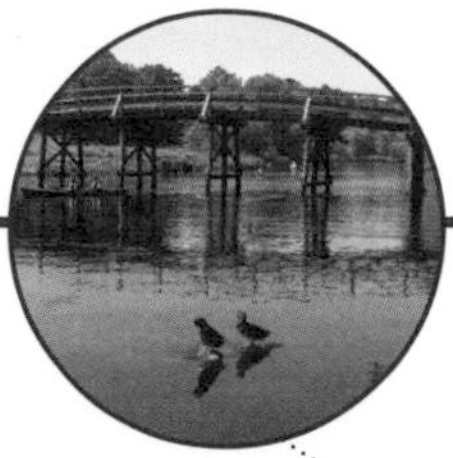

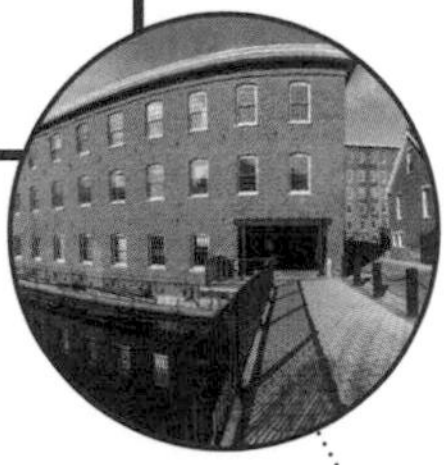

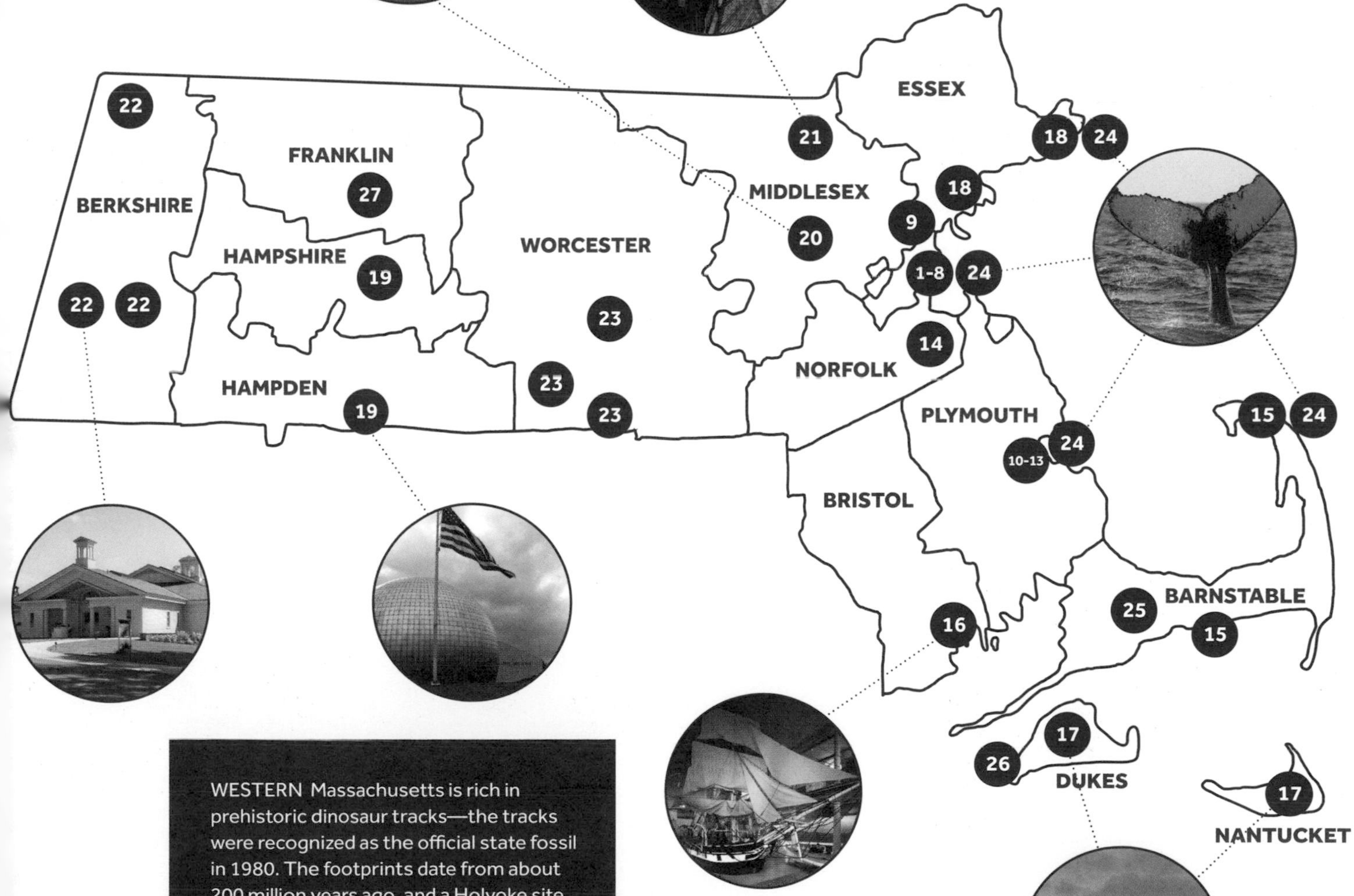
ESSEX
MIDDLESEX
FRANKLIN
BERKSHIRE
HAMPSHIRE
WORCESTER
HAMPDEN
NORFOLK
PLYMOUTH
BRISTOL
BARNSTABLE
DUKES
NANTUCKET
22
22
22
27
19
19
23
23
23
21
20
18
18
24
9
1-8
24
14
24
10-13
15
24
16
25
15
17
26
17

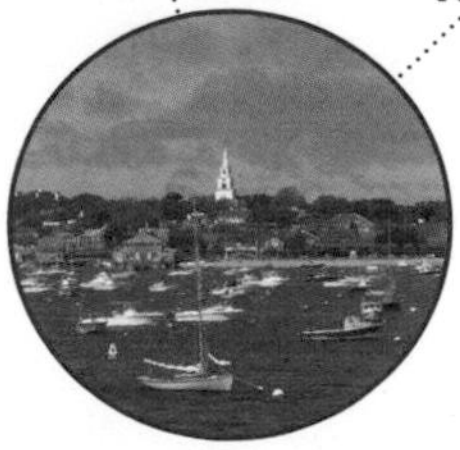

WESTERN Massachusetts is rich in prehistoric dinosaur tracks—the tracks were recognized as the official state fossil in 1980. The footprints date from about 200 million years ago, and a Holyoke site is one major attraction. The prints of a theropod dinosaur 50 feet in length from head to tail were found in nearby Granby, one of the most remarkable records of a theropod of such size.

PLACES TO VISIT

1. Massachusetts State House

The state capitol building in Boston, topped with its sparkling, golden dome, was completed in 1798 and designed by Charles Bulfinch. This stunning structure, which was constructed on Beacon Hill, houses the governor's offices and the General Court, the government body that makes the state's laws. Hanging above the House of Representatives chamber is the "Sacred Cod," a symbol of the early fishing industry.

2. The Freedom Trail

This 2.5-mile heritage route includes: Boston Common, where British soldiers once camped; Granary Burying Ground, the resting place of John Hancock, Samuel Adams, and Paul Revere; the Old State House, site of the Boston Massacre; Faneuil Hall, site of protests against British taxes; Paul Revere's House; the Bunker Hill Monument; and, among other sites, the historic warship USS *Constitution*.

3. Boston African-American National Historic Site

Explore the 19th-century free African-American community on Beacon Hill, a center of the national movement to end slavery. Along the Black Heritage Trail, visit the 1806 African Meeting House, the nation's oldest standing African-American church, and the Abiel Smith School. Don't miss the striking bronze memorial to the heroism of Colonel Robert Gould Shaw and the 54th Massachusetts Volunteers, an African-American military regiment that fought with distinction during the Civil War.

4. Commonwealth Museum and Massachusetts Archive

Dedicated to the history of Massachusetts, this Boston museum includes a fascinating Treasures Gallery featuring the royal charter of the Massachusetts Bay Colony and the Massachusetts Constitution, drafted by John Adams; Paul Revere's 1770 copperplate used to create the famous image of the Boston Massacre; and one of the original copies of the Declaration of Independence.

5. John F. Kennedy Presidential Library and Museum

Located on the Boston waterfront, this museum honors the legacy of JFK, the 35th U.S. President. Here you can tour a replica of the Oval Office, the president's office inside the White House. Nearby is the Edward M. Kennedy Institute for the United States Senate. Inside, visitors become "Senators-in-Training" and there is even a life-size copy of the U.S. Senate chamber.

6. Boston Tea Party Ships and Museum

Travel back in time and be a part of the Boston Tea Party, which helped launch the American Revolution. Board a full-scale copy of an 18th-century ship and throw tea overboard into Boston Harbor, just like the revolutionaries did more than 200 years ago. One of the museum's oldest artifacts is the Robinson Tea Chest, the only known surviving chest from the Boston Tea Party. A documentary dramatizes the events of April 19, 1775, including Paul Revere's famous "Midnight Ride."

7. Museum of Science

This popular Boston museum is located in Science Park, which spans the Charles River. It features interactive exhibits and activities, many of which are designed for children, and live presentations and shows at the Charles Hayden Planetarium. Other downtown sites include the world-class Museum of Fine Arts, Dreamland Wax Museum, and Skywalk Observatory.

8. The New England Holocaust Memorial

Located near the Freedom Trail, this Boston memorial honors the Jewish people killed by the Nazis during the Holocaust. Erected in 1995, and inspired by a group of Holocaust survivors, the memorial consists of six luminous glass towers which are lit internally from top to bottom. Engraved on the outside walls of each tower are numbers representing the six million Jews killed in the Holocaust.

9. Cambridge

Across the Charles River from Boston, you'll find the city of Cambridge, home to Harvard—one of the world's top universities and the oldest institution of higher learning in the United States. Take a walking tour of Harvard Yard—the university campus's historic center—or visit the popular Harvard Museum of Natural History. The Peabody Museum of Archeology and Ethnology includes an exhibition devoted to Native American cultures. Also in Cambridge is the Massachusetts Institute of Technology's MIT Museum.

10. 1620 Legacy Trail

As part of the Plymouth 400 commemoration of the *Mayflower* voyage, plans are underway to develop a 115-mile trail along the Massachusetts coast that will tell the shared history of the Pilgrims and Native American peoples. Among the places to visit will be Pilgrim Monument and Provincetown Museum, First Encounter Beach in Eastham, the Aquinnah Wampanoag Site and Pilgrim Hall Museum in Plymouth.

11. Plymouth Waterfront

At State Pier, board Plimoth Plantation's *Mayflower*, a full-scale reproduction of the ship that brought the Pilgrims to Plymouth in 1620. Also on the waterfront is Plymouth Rock, identified more than a century later as the Pilgrims' possible landing site. The rock broke in two in an attempt to change its location in 1774. Today, it sits on the shore beneath a classical-style structure.

12. Pilgrim Hall Museum

This fascinating Plymouth museum tells the story of the Pilgrims and Plymouth Colony. Learn, too, the story of the Native Wampanoag people who inhabited the area long before the arrival of European settlers. It also boasts a first-class collection of artifacts from the Pilgrims' lives, including the Bible of governor William Bradford, the sword of military adviser Myles Standish, and the great chair of William Brewster, the colony's religious leader.

13. Plimoth Plantation

One of the nation's premier "living museums" explores life in Wampanoag Patuxet and Plymouth Colony. A Wampanoag Homesite focuses on the ancient traditions of the region's Native people. In the 17th-century English Village, role-players represent the lives of actual residents of early Plymouth by speaking, acting, and dressing in the style of the 1620s. The museum includes a reproduction of the *Mayflower* and Plimoth Grist Mill.

14. South Shore

In addition to Plymouth, the South Shore boasts the Adams National Historical Park In Quincy. The historic Peacefield building was the home of the famous Massachusetts statesman, attorney and diplomat John Adams; who took office as the second U.S. President in 1797, his wife, Abigail; and later, of their son, John Quincy Adams, who became the sixth U.S. President in 1825.

15. Cape Cod

This beautiful peninsula is famous for its stunning National Seashore. In 1620, the Pilgrims signed the historic Mayflower Compact off what is now Provincetown, and the Pilgrim Monument and Provincetown Museum commemorate the event. The Whydah Pirate Museum is a must-see for families and, in the fall, don't miss a tour of the cranberry bogs, where early cranberry cultivation began.

16. New Bedford Whaling Museum

The New Bedford Whaling Museum has been collecting historic artifacts, documents, books, and photographs for more than 110 years and now boasts a varied collection of approximately 750,000 items. It holds one of the world's largest ship models, called the *Lagoda*—an 89-foot model of a whaling bark, or sailboat. Witness the fascinating story of the whaling industry and see thousands of pieces of scrimshaw—intricate designs on whale ivory.

17. Nantucket and Martha's Vineyard

These islands off the coast of Cape Cod were originally inhabited by Wampanoag people and later settled by the English. In the 19th century, they were centers of the whaling industry, made famous by the novel *Moby Dick*. It's thought "Martha" was the female relative of an English explorer. Native people still live there, many in the town of Aquinnah, which means "land under the hill."

18. Salem and the North Shore

Historic Salem was home to the infamous witch trials of the 17th century, though it was also an early seaport of Puritan New England and birthplace of the U.S. National Guard. The Salem Witch Museum recreates the horrors of the trials in a show not for the faint-hearted. The city of Gloucester is a popular center for whale watching. Gazing out of the harbor, the "Man at the Wheel" statue—a fisherman dressed in oilskins—is a symbol of the city.

19. Springfield

The city and surrounding area is full of fascinating places to visit. Springfield Armory National Historic Site highlights the nation's first armory. The Naismith Memorial Basketball Hall of Fame tells the story of James Naismith, who invented basketball in Springfield. The Dr. Seuss National Memorial Sculpture Garden celebrates local writer and illustrator Theodor Geisel. The Emily Dickinson Museum, including the poet's birthplace and home, is in Amherst.

20. Lexington and Concord

Along with nearby Concord, Lexington is considered a "birthplace of American liberty." On April 19, 1775, colonial militia battled British redcoats here, launching the Revolutionary War. View the Minuteman Statue on Lexington Battle Green and Buckman Tavern, where the militia gathered. Concord, too, played a major role at the start of the war. Visit the North Bridge, where "the shot heard round the world" was fired during the Battle of Concord.

21. Lowell National Historical Park

At this "living monument" to America's Industrial Revolution, you can learn about the "Mill Girls" and immigrant families who helped to make the city an important industrial center in the 19th century. Lowell's manufacturing facilities were planned as a reaction to the cramped and unhealthy living conditions for mill workers in Britain.

22. The Berkshires

This mountainous region in western Massachusetts is famous for arts and recreation. Its cultural highlights include the Norman Rockwell Museum in Stockbridge; the Massachusetts Museum of Contemporary Art in North Adams; the Clark Art Institute in Williamstown; Tanglewood music venue, where the Boston Symphony Orchestra plays in the summer; and Jacob's Pillow in Becket, said to be the oldest international summer dance festival in the U.S.

23. Worcester

Worcester boasts one of America's best art museums as well as the EcoTarium, a science and nature museum. Lake Chargoggagoggman-chauggagoggchaubunagungamaugg lies south of the city. This 45-letter place-name belongs to one of the largest lakes in Massachusetts. Old Sturbridge Village, located between Worcester and Springfield, allows visitors to experience life in a rural New England town of the 1830s on a scenic, 200-acre site.

24. Whale Watching

Massachusetts is famous for whale watching. Head for Stellwagen Bank National Marine Sanctuary —a feeding ground for whales, dolphins, and seabirds. Tour vessels operate from numerous departure points, including Boston, Gloucester, Provincetown, and Plymouth. If you are lucky, you will see many species of whales, including humpbacks, minkes, and pilot whales.

25. Mashpee Wampanoag Museum

This interesting and important museum records the history and culture of the Wampanoag from the Stone Age to the present day. Located in Mashpee, Cape Cod, the museum's exhibits include ancient artifacts and Native American heirlooms, including tools, baskets, hunting and fishing implements, weapons, and domestic utensils. The focal point is an impressive diorama depicting life in an early Wampanoag settlement.

26. Aquinnah Cultural Center

The Wampanoag Indian Museum in Aquinnah on Martha's Vineyard is housed in a historic Wampanoag family home. Its mission is to "preserve, interpret and document the Aquinnah Wampanoag's self-defined history, culture and contributions, past, present, and future." The museum showcases a number of fascinating Wampanoag artifacts, dating from the 17th century. In the summer, it hosts a popular festival of Native American crafts.

27. Historic Deerfield

Not far from Springfield in western Massachusetts, Historic Deerfield is a "living museum" of art, history, and architecture housed in 18th- and 19th-century buildings— including the 1884 Deerfield Inn—which line a mile-long street first laid out in 1671. Inside, visitors can discover a fascinating collection of art and antiques.

FLAGS OF MASSACHUSETTS

1. RED ENSIGN

This colonial flag, flown by the Massachusetts Bay Colony in the 17th century, displayed in its upper left corner the Cross of Saint George—patron saint of England. In another version, the Puritans removed the cross for religious reasons. A flag flown by the Province of Massachusetts Bay in the 18th century replaced the cross with the "Union Flag" of Great Britain.

2. PINE TREE

At the 1775 Battle of Bunker Hill, some believe the patriots of the American Revolution flew a flag with a green pine tree in the upper left corner. Ships commissioned under George Washington's Continental Army flew a pine tree flag as did the Massachusetts Navy. The motto, "An Appeal to Heaven," proclaimed the right to revolution.

3. GRAND UNION

Considered the first U.S. national flag, the Grand Union Flag of 1775 consisted of the 13 red and white stripes that remain on the flag today, representing the 13 British colonies, including Massachusetts. The upper left corner displayed the British Union Flag of that period. It signified the colonies' hope at that time of remaining attached to Britain.

4. AMERICAN

In 1777, the Second Continental Congress—which governed the newly independent colonies—stated that the U.S. flag would have "13 stripes, alternate red and white," and that "13 stars, white in a blue field," would represent the union of the colonies. The white is said to signify purity; red valor; and blue vigilance and justice. Today, the U.S. flag has 50 stars, one for each of the 50 states.

5. MASSACHUSETTS

The state coat of arms shows a blue shield, a white star and a Native American holding a bow and arrow—pointed down to signify peace. The state motto says: "By the sword we seek peace, but peace only under liberty." At the top, a bent arm holds a sword with the blade turned up—a reminder that the American Revolution won independence for the nation. The state flag was officially adopted in 1908.

THE MASSACHUSETTS COMPROMISE

THE MASSACHUSETTS Compromise was an important political agreement brokered by two famous Massachusetts statesmen, John Hancock and Samuel Adams. It helped lead to the ratification of the U.S. Constitution in 1788 and the Bill of Rights in 1791. During this period, there were heated debates in several U.S. states about whether to ratify the U.S. Constitution. Anti-federalists were worried that the Constitution would over-centralize government and restrict individual liberties. Federalists argued that the Constitution should be ratified without further amendment. The Massachusetts Compromise found an acceptable middle ground: the state would ratify the Constitution while also proposing future amendments including a Bill of Rights. Other states followed Hancock and Adams' lead. Arguably neither the U.S. Constitution nor the Bill of Rights would have been ratified in their final form had it not been for the Massachusetts Compromise.

THANKSGIVING

THE PILGRIMS will be forever associated with the Thanksgiving holiday. Just as the people of Plymouth celebrated their first harvest in 1621 with their Native allies, each Thanksgiving, Americans gather together to eat and express their gratitude. New Englanders kept this tradition alive in the 1600s and 1700s. At the urging of writer and editor Sarah Josepha Hale, Abraham Lincoln declared a national Thanksgiving for November 1863, during the Civil War. In the years following the Great Depression, the fourth Thursday in November was confirmed as Thanksgiving Day. In 1970, drawing attention to the changes brought by colonization, some Native Americans began observing Thanksgiving as a Day of Mourning.

SAMUEL ADAMS AND PAUL REVERE TIME CAPSULE

A CORNERSTONE of the Massachusetts State House contains the Samuel Adams and Paul Revere Time Capsule, believed to have been buried in 1795, and one of the oldest such capsules in the U.S. Originally in a leather pouch, it was rehoused in a metal box, then an archival container. The contents included newspaper pages from the time period, a copper medal that belonged to George Washington, a 1652 "pine tree" shilling, and other money.

GOVERNMENT OF MASSACHUSETTS

MASSACHUSETTS has three main branches of state government

EXECUTIVE

The governor is head of the executive branch with the power to activate the Commonwealth's military forces called the National Guard. Elected for a four-year term, the governor is in charge of several large state agencies. Other important elected officials include the Lieutenant Governor and Secretary of the Commonwealth.

LEGISLATIVE

State laws are enacted by the General Court, the state legislature based in the capital city of Boston. The General Court is made up of 160 members of the state's House of Representatives and 40 members of the Senate, who all serve two-year terms.

JUDICIAL

The state judiciary, or court system, applies the laws of Massachusetts. The Supreme Judicial Court dates back to colonial times and oversees all the state's courts, which handle criminal cases and civil lawsuits. The governor, with the consent of an elected Governor's Council, appoints Massachusetts judges.

LOCAL GOVERNMENT

Most county governments have been abolished in favor of cities and towns granted authority over local issues and, for some, a measure of "home rule."

U.S. GOVERNMENT

The powers of the federal national government—originally created for collective defense of the states, and foreign diplomacy—are placed in the President, U.S. Congress, and the U.S. Supreme Court in a system of "checks and balances." Congress has 435 voting members of the U.S. House of Representatives—nine from Massachusetts—and 100 elected members of the U.S. Senate, two from each of the 50 states.

Massachusetts is one of the few U.S. states to be called a "Commonwealth"—a term used by John Adams when framing the Massachusetts Constitution that was popular at the time to describe a whole body of people making up a state or nation.

MASSACHUSETTS HONOR ROLL

Massasoit
(?–1661)

Wampanoag sachem leader whose alliance with the Pilgrims of Plymouth Colony lasted throughout his lifetime.

John Carver
(?–1621)

A Pilgrim said to be the first signer of the Mayflower Compact who became the colony's first governor.

Tisquantum
(?–1622)

Native man who learned to speak English after being kidnapped. He became the Pilgrims' guide and interpreter.

John Winthrop
(1588–1649)

Lawyer who brought Puritans to the Massachusetts Bay Colony and became the colony's most influential governor.

William Blackstone
(1595–1675)

Englishman credited as the first European settler in what became the city of Boston.

John Harvard
(1607–1638)

English clergyman who helped to fund Harvard College, now one of the world's top universities.

Caleb Cheeshahteau-muck (c.1644–1666)

Born on Martha's Vineyard, the Wampanoag man became the first Native American to graduate from Harvard.

Samuel Whittemore
(1696–1793)

At age 78, the Charlestown-born farmer became the oldest known combatant in the Revolutionary War.

Samuel Adams
(1722–1803)

American Revolution leader and signer of the Declaration of Independence, who became a governor of Massachusetts.

Paul Revere
(1735–1818)

American Revolution hero, famous for his "midnight ride" to warn colonists that the British redcoats were coming.

John Adams
(1735–1826)

Second U.S. President, signed the Declaration of Independence, and authored the Massachusetts Constitution.

John Hancock
(1737–1793)

Continental Congress president who signed the Declaration of Independence. First governor of Massachusetts.

Abigail Adams
(1744–1818)

Wife of John Adams and mother of John Quincy Adams—both U.S. presidents—and an early advocate of women's rights.

Henry Knox
(1750–1806)

A military officer who played a key role in securing cannons for George Washington's victory at the Siege of Boston.

Phillis Wheatley
(1753–1784)

A former slave, she was the first African-American female poet to be published in America and Britain.

Deborah Sampson
(1760–1827)

A Plympton-born woman who dressed as a man to serve in the Continental Army during the Revolutionary War.

John Quincy Adams
(1767–1848)

Son of John and Abigail Adams and U.S. Senator from Massachusetts, who became the sixth U.S. President.

Dorcas Honorable
(c. 1770–1855)

Nantucket Wampanoag who was indentured to a sea captain. The mark on her right cheek is a slave brand.

GLOSSARY

Here are definitions for concepts found in *The Massachusetts Chronicles*, including words marked in red on the timeline.

Abolition movement Campaign to end slavery

Amendment An article added to the U.S. Constitution to change existing laws

Assassinated Killed for political or religious reasons

Bill of Rights First ten amendments to the U.S. Constitution

Busing Transporting students to schools within or outside their local school districts to reduce racial segregation

Charter By which a city, colony or other body is founded, or its rights and privileges defined

Colonization When a group of people create a settlement, i.e. living near each other in a foreign place, and governing it

Compact Agreement between one or more parties

Constitution Basic principles of law governing a nation or state

Continental Army Formed by the Second Continental Congress, it led the colonies' military revolt against British rule

Continental Congress Convention of delegates from 13 colonies that governed the U.S. during the American Revolution

Declaration of Independence Declaration by the Second Continental Congress that the 13 American colonies were now independent from Britain

Emancipate To free a slave or other disadvantaged person

Evangelical According to the teaching of the Gospel in the Bible

MASSACHUSETTS HONOR ROLL

Francis Cabot Lowell (1775–1817)

Pioneer of the Industrial Revolution, especially the textile industry in Massachusetts. Lowell is named for him.

Sarah Josepha Hale (1788–1879)

Author of the nursery rhyme "Mary Had a Little Lamb," who campaigned for Thanksgiving to be a national holiday.

Lucretia Mott (1793–1880)

Quaker abolitionist, born in Nantucket, who helped organize the historic women's rights convention in Seneca Falls, New York.

George Peabody (1795–1869)

Businessman and philanthropist, known for his wide-ranging charitable work in America and Britain.

Sojourner Truth (c. 1797–1883)

African-American abolitionist and former slave who won a court case against a white man to recover her enslaved son.

Charles Goodyear (1800–1860)

Inventor who created waterproof, moldable rubber while in Woburn, making tires and rubber footwear possible.

Nathaniel Hawthorne (1804–1864)

Salem-born writer, whose famous novel *The Scarlet Letter* is inspired by Puritan New England.

Emily Dickinson (1830–1886)

World-famous writer from Amherst whose poetry, written mainly in private, was revealed only after her death.

Robert Gould Shaw (1837–1863)

White military officer who led African-American soldiers of the 54th Massachusetts, killed in the Civil War.

William Harvey Carney (1840–1908)

African-American soldier of the 54th Massachusetts, awarded the Medal of Honor for his heroism during the Civil War.

Alexander Graham Bell (1847–1922)

Boston professor who invented the first practical telephone, transforming communications around the world.

Anne Sullivan (1866–1936)

Agawam-born teacher who taught deaf-blind Helen Keller (left), despite suffering periods of blindness herself.

Emily Greene Balch (1867–1961)

Boston-born economist who won the Nobel Peace Prize as a leader of the Women's International League for Peace and Freedom.

W. E. B. Du Bois (1868–1963)

Civil rights activist and author who cofounded the National Association for the Advancement of Colored People.

Calvin Coolidge (1872–1933)

Mayor of Northampton, governor of Massachusetts, U.S. Vice President, and 30th U.S. President.

Frances Perkins (1880–1965)

Boston-born U.S. secretary of labor, the first woman appointed to the U.S. President's Cabinet—made up of senior advisers.

John Hays Hammond, Jr. (1888–1965)

Inventor and friend of Alexander Graham Bell who pioneered electronic remote control and built a castle in Gloucester.

George Belain (c.1893–1918)

Great-grandson of a whaler, this Aquinnah Wampanoag soldier died in combat at the age of 25 in World War I in France.

Founding Fathers A group of politicians, philosophers, and writers who led the American Revolution

Fowl Poultry or game birds kept for their eggs and meat

French and Indian War Battle between Britain and France over territory in North America, where they were fighting for supremacy, 1754–1763

Indentured servants Workers who are bound to an employer for a fixed time, before gaining their freedom

Indigenous Native to a particular place

Industrial Revolution Period of technological advancement and social change, including the growth of factories and new engines powered by steam

Integration Effort to create equal opportunities for people of all races by ending racial segregation (see below)

Martyrs People killed because of their religious or other beliefs

Massachusetts Bay Company Trading company given a charter by the English Crown to colonize an area of New England. It was taken over by Puritans seeking to establish a religious community

Militia Non-professional soldiers who are citizens of a state or nation

Minutemen (Minute Men) Colonial fighting men in the American Revolution, who were ready for service at any time

Patent Government license protecting an original invention from being copied by others

Patriots American colonists who fought for independence from British rule

Pike A weapon comprising a long wooden shaft with a pointed iron or steel head

Privateers Armed ships owned by individuals but authorized by governments for use in war

MASSACHUSETTS HONOR ROLL

George Dilboy (1896–1918)

Greek-American soldier in the 26th "Yankee" Division, awarded a Medal of Honor for his heroism in World War I.

"Tip" O'Neill (1912–1994)

Cambridge-born politician, one of the longest-serving Speakers of the U.S. House of Representatives.

John F. Kennedy (1917–1963)

"JFK," the U.S. Senator and Congressman from Massachusetts became the 35th U.S. President. He was assassinated in 1963.

Leonard Bernstein (1918–1990)

Lawrence-born conductor who composed the music for *West Side Story*, one of America's greatest musicals.

Ted Williams (1918–2002)

Considered one of baseball's greats, Williams played for the Boston Red Sox for a total of 19 years.

An Wang (1920–1990)

Chinese-American inventor and philanthropist who established a Massachusetts computer company.

Rocky Marciano (1923–1969)

Born and raised in Brockton, he was the undefeated world heavyweight boxing champion during the 1950s.

Frank "Wamsutta" James (1923–2001)

Wampanoag elder who in 1970 declared Thanksgiving a "National Day of Mourning" after his speech was censored.

George H. W. Bush (1924–2018)

The Milton-born oil man and World War II veteran became the 41st President of the United States.

Robert F. Kennedy (1925–1968)

Brookline-born politician, U.S. Attorney General, and civil rights supporter. Assassinated, like his brother JFK.

Edward M. Kennedy (1932–2009)

The youngest brother of JFK and RFK represented Massachusetts in the U.S. Senate for almost 47 years.

Michael Dukakis (1933–)

Greek-American Governor of Massachusetts, the longest-serving in the state, who lost a U.S. presidential campaign.

Bill Russell (1934–)

One of the greatest basketball players, he won an Olympic gold medal and 11 NBA championships with the Boston Celtics.

Nelson Merced (1947–)

The first Hispanic to serve in the Massachusetts state legislature, he campaigned for Boston schools.

Deval Patrick (1956–)

Only African-American to serve as Governor of Massachusetts— from 2007 to 2015— who also attended Harvard Law School.

Stephanie Wilson (1966–)

The Boston-born and Harvard-educated astronaut flew on three Space Shuttle missions, spending 42 days in space.

Tom Brady (1977–)

New England Patriots quarterback who won six Super Bowls, the most of any player in football history.

Aly Raisman (1994–)

Needham-born gymnast who won two Olympic gold medals in 2012 and one in 2016.

Puritans English Protestants who sought to "purify" or reform the Church of England from within, simplifying forms of worship and religious practice

Quakers Members of a Christian movement who reject conventional forms of worship and historically advocate pacifism

Reconstruction Period when U.S. government controlled defeated Confederate states and ended slavery

Redcoats British soldiers in America during the Revolutionary War

Sachem Among some Native peoples, a leader or chief

Segregation Separation of people due to their race or nationality

Separatists English Protestants who left the Church of England because they felt it could not be reformed enough for them to remain within it. Many of the first English people to come to Plymouth were Separatists

Spectral evidence Evidence based on dreams and "visions"

State capitol The main state government building, not to be confused with the state capital, the seat of state government

Suffragist Campaigner for women's right to vote

Transcendentalist Someone who believes godliness can be found in all nature and humanity

Trespass To enter someone's land or property without permission

Tyranny Cruel and unfair government in which all power is in the hands of one ruler

Union Federal union of states during the Civil War

"War of the Currents" Events relating to competing electric power systems—alternating current (AC) and direct current (DC)—and their adoption in the U.S.

Weirs Enclosures or fences set in a waterway to catch fish, a technique mastered by Native American peoples

PRIMARY SOURCES

Pages 1–8 *The Common Pot.* By Lisa Brooks

Page 2 *The Voyage of Archangell: James Rosier's Account of the Weymouth Voyage of 1605, A True Relation.* By James Rosier

Page 2 *A Briefe Narration of the Originall Undertakings of the Advancement of Plantations Into the Parts of America: Especially Shewing the Beginning, Progress and Continuance of that of New-England.* By Sir Ferdinando Gorges

Page 2 *John Smith's Map of New England, 1616.* By Captain John Smith

Pages 4–6 *Mourt's Relation (A Relation or Journal of the Beginning and Proceedings of the English Plantation Settled at Plimoth in New England).* By Edward Winslow and William Bradford

Pages 4–6 *Of Plymouth Plantation.* By William Bradford

Page 7 *A Model of Christian Charity.* By John Winthrop

Page 9 *On Witchcraft.* By Cotton Mather

Page 15 *The Adams-Jefferson Letters: The Complete Correspondence Between Thomas Jefferson and Abigail and John Adams.* Edited by Lester J. Cappon

Page 16 *A Discourse Delivered on the Death of Capt. Paul Cuffee.* By Reverend Peter Williams

Page 19 *Narrative of the Life of Frederick Douglass, an American Slave.* By Frederick Douglass

Page 20 *Keetsahnak: Our Missing and Murdered Indigenous Sisters.* Edited by Kim Anderson et al

Page 23 *The Invention of "Basket Ball".* By James Naismith

Page 23 *The Story of My Life.* By Helen Keller

Page 26 *The Cat in the Hat by Dr. Seuss.* Written and illustrated by Theodor Seuss Geisel

Page 27 *Profiles in Courage.* By John F. Kennedy

Page 27 *Wind in the Fire.* By Bobbi Gibb

Page 28 *The Suppressed Speech of Wamsutta (Frank) James, Wampanoag.* By Wamsutta (Frank) James

Page 30 *Ruth Wakefield's Toll House Tried and True Recipes.* By Ruth Graves Wakefield

FURTHER READING

Our Beloved Kin, *Lisa Brooks*

The Common Pot, *Lisa Brooks*

Braiding Sweetgrass, *Robin Wall Kimmerer*

Sacred Instructions, *Sherri Mitchell*

An Indigenous Peoples' History of the United States for Young People, *Roxanne Dunbar-Ortiz*

North America, A Fold-Out Graphic History, *Sarah Albee*

The Mayflower: A Story of Courage, Community, and War, *Nathaniel Philbrick*

A Short History of Boston, *Robert J. Allison*

Boston in the American Revolution, A Town Versus an Empire, *Brooke Barbier*

Hidden History of Boston, *Dina Vargo*

Boston History for Kids, *Richard Panchyk*

ABOUT THE AUTHORS

Linda Coombs is a member of the Aquinnah Wampanoag tribe on Martha's Vineyard, and has lived in Mashpee for more than 40 years. Both of her grandchildren are enrolled with the Mashpee Wampanoag tribe, as was their father and grandfather. Linda has worked for 45 years as a museum educator, spending 11 years in total at the Boston Children's Museum, 30 years in the Wampanoag Indigenous Program of Plimoth Plantation, and nine years at the Aquinnah Cultural Center, a small house museum representing Aquinnah Wampanoag history. She has been an interpreter, an artisan, a researcher; led workshops and teacher institutes; and written children's stories and articles on various aspects of Wampanoag history and culture.

Mark Skipworth studied Modern History at St. John's, Oxford University, and was a senior newspaper editor at *The Sunday Times* in London. At the *Daily Telegraph* and *Sunday Telegraph* in London he was Executive Editor and later Deputy Editor. As a reporter, he won a number of prestigious media awards for campaigns and investigations. Mark has a passion for history and has chaired numerous events at literary festivals in Britain and internationally. He has written several nonfiction works, including two other U.S. state histories: *The Illinois Chronicles* and *The Texas Chronicles*.

First published in 2020 by What on Earth Books LLC, 30 Ridge Road Unit B, Greenbelt, Maryland. 20770.
Copyright © 2020 What on Earth Books

Acknowledgments: This book would have been impossible without the help and support of a large group of people, all of whom are passionate about history and civics education. We would especially like to thank concept creator and editor-in-chief, Christopher Lloyd. Additional research and writing by Julie Deegan and Andrew Pettie. Editing by Laura Marchant. Design by Grade Design, Andy Forshaw, and Daisy Symes. Picture research by Felicity Page. Editorial contributions and additional thanks to: Michele Pecoraro, Gary Maestas, Rob Powers, Tricia Liskov, Vinny deMacedo, Brian Logan, Charles Wall, Donna Curtin, Rob Kluin, Cedric Woods, Tom Begley, Kate LaPrad, Stephen Kenney, John Buckley, Rebecca Griffith, Michelle Ryan, Cheryll Toney Holley, Larry Mann, Jessie Little Doe Baird, Fred Clark, Deniz Leuenberger, Paul Jean, Jo Hoffman, Tom Nestor, Steve Zuromski, Eric LePage, Kayla DaCosta, Alyssa Asci, Brenda Molife, Bruce Bartlett, Patricia Bartlett, and Alice Richmond.

Library of Congress Cataloging-in-Publication Data available upon request.
ISBN: 978-1-9998028-0-6
10 9 8 7 6 5 4 3 2 1
whatonearthbooks.com